WEB RESEARCH

WEB RESEARCH

Selecting, Evaluating, and Citing

MARIE L. RADFORD
Pratt Institute

SUSAN B. BARNES
Fordham University

LINDA R. BARR
University of the Virgin Islands

/6010/

Allyn and Bacon

Boston ▪ London ▪ Toronto ▪ Sydney ▪ Tokyo ▪ Singapore

Senior Editor: Karon Bowers
Editorial Assistant: Jennifer Trebby
Marketing Manager: Mandee Eckersley
Editorial-Production Service: Omegatype Typography, Inc.
Manufacturing Buyer: Julie McNeill
Cover Administrator: Kristina Mose-Libon
Electronic Composition: Omegatype Typography, Inc.

Library of Congress Cataloging-in-Publication Data

Radford, Marie L.
   Web research : selecting, evaluating, and citing / Marie L. Radford, Susan B. Barnes,
Linda R. Barr.
      p. cm.
Includes bibliographical references and index.
ISBN 0-205-33249-8
   1. Internet searching. 2. Computer network resources—Evaluation. 3. Citation of
electronic information resources. I. Barnes, Susan B. II. Barr, Linda R. (Linda
Robinson) III. Title.

ZA4201 .R33 2002
025.04—dc21

                                                                          2001041264

Printed in the United States of America
10 9 8 7 6 5 4 3   06 05 04 03

CONTENTS

●●

....

CHAPTER SIX

When and How to Cite Web Sources   81

TABLES

● ●

PREFACE

With the widespread use of the Internet, the World Wide Web has become a centralizing network from which to collect, distribute, and locate information for personal, educational, and scholarly use. Currently, students are using the Web as a research source in addition to, and often in place of, traditional printed texts. As more students use the Web as a source of information, they are faced with the problem of how to evaluate critically the information they find. This book was written to help students more effectively select, evaluate, and cite web information. It was developed as a reference text for use by undergraduate and graduate students majoring in a wide variety of subjects. Toward this end all terms that are boldface are defined in the Glossary at the end of the book.

Web Research: Selecting, Evaluating, and Citing brings together a librarian, a cybrarian, and a visual communicator to examine the critical issues associated with using the World Wide Web as a scholarly research tool. The book includes the following topics: understanding when to use the Web as a research tool, locating credible information, critically evaluating websites (both visually and verbally), avoiding plagiarism and copyright problems, and citing web references. By developing guidelines, this book helps students more effectively use the Web as a research tool for the twenty-first century.

ACKNOWLEDGMENTS

Behind the scenes, there are many people who contribute to the creation of a book. First and foremost, we thank our editor, Karon Bowers, for understanding the importance of this book. Additionally, Sarah Kelly and Rebecca Sullivan, editorial assistants at Allyn and Bacon/Longman, deserve special recognition for orchestrating the review and production processes for this project. Dean Robert Himmelberg needs to be acknowledged because he provided research support through a Fordham University Ames Grant for this project. Research assistants Yvette Mena and Grace Ekanem spent tireless hours searching the Web for critical evaluation sites. We thank them for their efforts.

Creating a book about the Web requires visuals. A special thanks goes to John Terhorst for his enthusiasm and creativity in bringing the Dot Com character to life through his wonderful illustrations. Additionally, we would like to thank all the companies, individuals, and organizations that allowed us to use screen captures of their websites, including the American Civil Liberties Union, The Library of Congress, the *New York Times*, Marie L. Radford, the Ralph M. Paiewonsky Library of the University of the Virgin Islands, Yahoo!, Northern Light Technology, Infospace, Inc., the David and Lorraine Cheng Library at the William Paterson University of New Jersey, Netscape, and Bob Drudge from Refdesk. Many thanks go to Kurt Wagner for allowing us to include his site, but, more important, for his continuing support throughout this project. He deserves special recognition.

In addition to the people mentioned above, each of us has her own group of people to thank. Marie L. Radford thanks her husband, Gary P. Radford, for reading drafts, for creating the index, and for his unflagging encouragement and love. Susan Barnes would like to thank her husband, Roger Berger, for his help throughout this project. Linda Robinson Barr thanks her parents for reading drafts and for their excitement about the project.

Finally, we would like to thank Terry Doyle, Northern Virginia Community College, and Marilyn Shaw, University of Northern Iowa, for reviewing the manuscript and contributing excellent suggestions for revisions.

CHAPTER 1

Using the Web as a Research Tool

Today's college or university students, like you, have an incredible range of information resources and services available through the World Wide Web (WWW). Since 1993, the WWW, a vast interconnected system of global information networks, has been accessible through Internet graphical **browsers,** such as Microsoft Internet Explorer and Netscape Navigator, to help students with research for course assignments.

WHAT THIS BOOK *IS* AND *IS NOT*

This book is designed to help you become web savvy—both efficient and effective in using the WWW to find the right quantity and highest-quality information you need for your course work and academic assignments. This book is *not* designed to help you find recreational information such as MP3s, the latest concert dates for your favorite rock band, or games.

As you probably are already aware, you can waste valuable study time and quickly become frustrated chasing around cyberspace, unable to zero in on the right website for your research. Before you know it, time quickly slips away while you search through pages full of links to potentially useful web pages, some of which seem to take forever to download. In the end, you are no closer to completing your assignment. This book gives you practical tips on how not to get caught in the World Wide "Cob Web"; on how to choose search engines, subject directories, and metasites; and especially on how to evaluate the information that you find. In addition, you can learn how to avoid violating copyright by properly citing web resources in papers and other assignments.

Now, for some basic information, followed by some good news and some bad news (Oh no!) about the WWW.

THE ROCK-BOTTOM BASICS

On a short deadline? WWW resources are instantly available to help you with class assignments. Web pages and databases provide many different types of valuable information, including

- Statistics
- Full-text journal and newspaper articles
- Library holdings
- Both U.S. and global government information
- Biographical information
- Dictionaries, encyclopedias, almanacs, and handbooks
- Quotations
- Graphics
- Directories
- Audio- and videoclips
- E-books and e-journals
- Maps and geographical information
- Stock quotes and company information

Some Basic Terminology

HTML. HTML **(hypertext markup language)** allows information on Web pages to be easily accessed and displayed.

URL. Each web page is located by a URL **(uniform resource locator),** which usually begins with http:// and which you can type into your browser in the Location box at the top.

Hyperlinks. **Hyperlinks** quickly connect you to other web pages, databases, and files. They are easily recognized and activated by text highlighted with color, underlining, or graphic buttons.

Good News!

WWW information is easy to download to a floppy or cut and paste into your word processing program. This information can be used for taking notes, writing papers, and preparing oral reports. A variety of **search engines,** specialized subject directories, and **metasites** are available to help you find your way to the best quality information the Web has to offer. The WWW can provide a much more efficient and effective way to search traditional resources, such as newspapers and journals. The WWW offers the following advantages, according to Berkman (2000):

- **Speed.** Doing web research can be quicker than doing research using paper sources.
- **Timeliness.** WWW resources can be more up to date than print materials.
- **Multimedia.** WWW includes audio, video, and graphics.
- **Hyperlinks.** With just a click you can move quickly to related websites.

More and more primary sources (e.g., government documents, speeches, letters, diaries, etc.) are becoming available through the Web. More and more authoritative reference sources (e.g., the *Encyclopedia Britannica*, www.britannica.com) are providing WWW access to their products, for a subscription fee. Others, like *Merriam-Webster's Collegiate Dictionary and Thesaurus*, (www.m-w.com) are free. These sources are usually supported through web advertisements. More and more universities are purchasing subscriptions to fee-based information services (e.g., ProQuest or Infotrac, which index high-quality full-text journal and newspaper articles on a variety of topics) for student use. You can often use these services both on and off campus. You can also access them through your university library home page.

Bad News! (But Don't Panic)

Although using the WWW has its pitfalls and obstacles, the upcoming chapters of this book help enable you to steer clear. Table 1.1 offers 10 essentials for doing research on the Web.

Information Overload! The vastness of the WWW is both a plus and a minus. About 99.99 percent of web resources are useless for obtaining serious research for class assignments. How do you find just the right piece of information you are looking for in billions of web pages?

Yee Haw! The WWW Is the Wild Wild Web! Although billions of web pages are packed full of information, no one is in charge of quality control. How do you know whether the web page you are using to write your research paper is the authoritative real deal or is written by someone's kid sister? Web pages are not permanent; they have a habit of being here today and gone tomorrow.

Search Engine Overload! So many search engines and metasites are available, how do you know which one to use? How do you best use a variety of basic and advanced features of search engines to find quickly what you need?

Advertisement Overload! The advertisements on search engines and reference resources can be really annoying. How can you best avoid them?

TABLE 1.1   Ten Essentials for Using the WWW for Research

THE ESSENTIALS	HERE'S MORE INFORMATION	WHAT TO DO
1. Your first stop is your library's home page.	Librarians at your campus have located and organized web and other online resources that are most likely to be of value to *you*. The library home page is a great place to start research for any project.	Check it out! Ask library personnel if you don't know your library's home page URL or need help in navigating.
2. The WWW is big, really, really big!	Any given search engine is only searching a *fraction* of the Web.	Use several search engines, or an **integrated search engine.**
3. Search engines have different features.	These unique features allow you to combine terms, search word variations, search phrases, search different parts of the Web (e.g., Usenet groups, etc.).	Use Help features (also, Search Tips, Power Searching, or Advanced Searching) when using unfamiliar search engines or when using a favorite search engine, because these engines are always being fine tuned.
4. Search engines only search words *not* concepts.	When you enter in the word *Java*, for example, the search engine looks for that *exact term*. It cannot tell the difference between *Java* (the programming language), *Java* (the country), or *Java* (the slang term for coffee).	Combine terms for better results. For example, use the words *Java AND Indonesia* or *Java NOT coffee* for information on the country.
5. Combining terms is more efficient when searching the WWW.	**Boolean operators,** such as **AND, OR, NOT,** can reduce the number of unrelated or unwanted websites you retrieve (also, **false hits**) and increase **precision.**	Always use Boolean operators. Check Help features for the search engine to see how they are used. For example, some search engines use the + sign instead of typing *AND*.
6. Search engines have different ways to determine **relevance** and order of output (that is, which pages appear first, second, etc.).	The search engine may simply count the number of times your term appears. However, other criteria can be used. (See the Tip on page 13.)	Check Help to find out how **relevance** is determined. Use meta-sites chosen by subject experts to cut down on commercial site retrieval.

(continued)

TABLE 1.1   (continued)

THE ESSENTIALS	HERE'S MORE INFORMATION	WHAT TO DO
7. GIGO stands for garbage in, garbage out.	GIGO means that just because something is on the Web, that does not make it true. Web content may be inaccurate if mistakes are made when inputting information, or if web page developers are careless or uninformed.	Be aware of the authority of the web page developer. Verify web information using another resource if possible. See Chapter 3 for more help in evaluating web content.
8. Let the searcher beware! *No one* edits web content.	Unlike this book or your text-books, no editorial team is checking facts and verifying information on the Web. Anyone, repeat *anyone* can put *anything* on the Web.	Be critical of web content and verify information. See Chapter 3 for more help in evaluating web content.
9. Know what you are searching.	Browsers search the entire Web to retrieve pages that match the exact URL you enter. Search engines search only a small portion of the Web. Some **metasearch engines** search the output of many other search engines. If you are searching an online library catalog, or a subscription database from your library's home page (e.g., ProQuest or EBSCOhost), you are only searching the contents of that database, not the Web at all.	Think before you search! Check search engine Help. Some search engines allow you to search specific portions of the Web (such as Usenets) or by **extensions** or **domains** (e.g., dot.com or dot.gov).
10. Know your limitations.	Don't assume that you are a super searcher. Even if you have done lots of web searching, new search engines and new resources are becoming available every day, and familiar ones may have changed overnight.	Be open to learning more about searching the Web! Don't be satisfied with the first site you find. Look for quality information.

Caution! Plagiarism Potential. Cite Your Site!   Because the information from the WWW is so easy to download or cut and paste into your word processor for writing papers, it is easy to forget to cite your sources or to keep track of direct quotes. (For more information on **plagiarism,** see Chapter 4.)

Where do you think that the savviest web searchers on your campus are to be found? Give up? They are in your campus library! That's right! Your *librarians,* easily found at the reference desk, are deeply involved in web searching, evaluation of resources, and selecting the highest quality websites for you to easily find on your library's home page. Some even have titles such as *cybrarian* or *library web developer.* Check your library's home page to see if they offer email or chat reference services that you can access from on or off campus. You can usually phone the library for immediate help too.

IDENTIFYING WEBSITES

When evaluating websites, it is helpful first to identify the type of site that you are viewing. Websites can be placed into six basic categories:

- Advocacy
- Business
- Informational
- News
- Personal
- Entertainment

Sometimes you can tell the type of site by looking at the web address, or uniform resource locator (URL). The URL is the address of the website. URLs contain information about where the file is located. Each web page has its own unique URL. The web address includes the **hypertext transport protocol (http),** the name of the server the page is located on (also called the **domain name**), the path or location of the page, and the name of the individual page. For example, all these bits of information are contained in the following URL: http://www.server.edu/ path/file_name.html.

Websites are created for a variety of different reasons (see Table 1.2). Identifying the purpose of the site helps you evaluate the credibility of the site. For example, a site designed to promote a product, as a television commercial does, will only say good things about it. Similarly, advocacy sites are created to convince you to support their cause. Knowing the point of view expressed by the site or its bias is important in determining the credibility of information.

Advocacy Sites.   Advocacy sites are created to influence public opinion or to encourage activism. The individuals, groups, or organizations that run these sites often attempt to increase membership in the organization. Examples include websites for the Democratic (www.democrats.org/) and Republican (www.rnc.org/) parties, the American Cancer Society (www.cancer.org), and the American Civil Liberties Union (www.aclu.org) (Figure 1.1).

TABLE 1.2   Types of Websites

TYPE	PURPOSE	URL ADDRESS
Advocacy	To influence public opinion	Frequently ends in .org
	To promote a cause	
	To promote a nonprofit organization	
Business	To promote a product or service	Frequently ends in .com
Informational	To provide factual information	Variety of endings, especially .edu and .org
News	To provide information about local, regional, national, or international news	Frequently ends in .com
Personal	To fulfill a variety of reasons for an individual	Variety of endings, especially .com and .edu
Entertainment	To provide enjoyment	Variety of endings

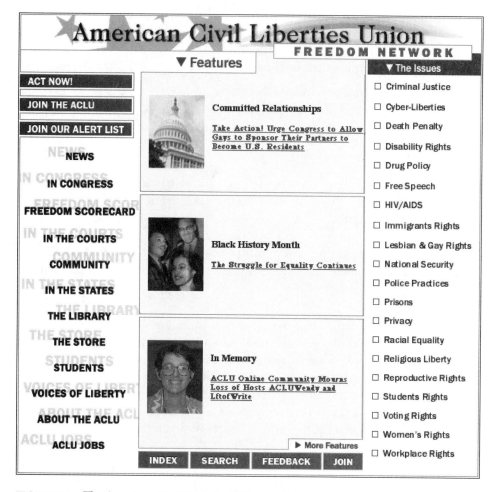

FIGURE 1.1 The American Civil Liberties Union website is an example of an advocacy site. Reprinted with permission from the American Civil Liberties Union.

In mid November, 2000, the Internet Corporation for Assigned Names and Numbers (ICANN) voted to add seven new top level domains which will be available in 2001. Additional information can be found on their website (www.icann.org).

NEW DOMAINS

.aero—air transportation industry

.biz—businesses

.coop—cooperatives

.info—unrestricted general use

.museums—museums

.name—individuals

.pro—certified professional and professional entities (doctors, lawyers, etc.)

Business Sites.   Business sites are constructed to promote a product or service. These sites may offer online sales catalogs, provide product documentation, distribute press releases and information about the company, offer electronic services, and provide customer support. Business sites generally have a marketing orientation and they may attempt to collect information from web users. Examples are Amazon (www.amazon.com) and Barnes and Noble (www.bn.com).

Information Sites.   Information sites are built to provide factual information such as government research reports, census data, transportation schedules, course schedules, and encyclopedia information. A variety of different information sites include everything from concert schedules to government databases. Examples include websites for your college or university, *Merriam-Webster's Collegiate Dictionary and Thesaurus* (www.m-w. com/dictionary.htm), and Fedstats (www.fedstats.gov) (see Figure 1.2).

News Sites.   News sites are often developed by traditional companies, including media such as newspapers, magazines, radio stations, television, and books. These websites often parallel the more traditional medium that they represent. For example, the CNN site has video- and audioclips from its television station. Your understanding of the traditional medium sponsoring the site can help you determine the credibility of the site. Examples include the *New York Times* (www.nytimes.com) (Figure 1.3), Cable News Network (www.cnn.com), and CNET (www. news.com).

Personal Sites.   Personal sites are designed by individuals for many reasons, including shameless self-promotion, presenting an online resume or portfolio, sharing creative talents such as illustration or writing, providing personal information about a family or personal activities, or providing information about a topic of interest. An example of a personal website is

FIGURE 1.2 The Library of Congress has an informational site that contains text, photographs, maps, graphics, moving images, and other American documents.

Reprinted with permission from the Library of Congress.

Marie L. Radford's site, which is located at pages.prodigy.net/mradford/ (see Figure 1.4).

Entertainment Sites. Entertainment sites are established to provide enjoyment to users. Entertainment sites may participate in producing parodies that satirize other websites. For example, www.whitehouse.net is a parody of the original White House site, located at www.whitehouse.gov. Other entertainment websites provide games, jokes, fan information, chat, and movie clips. Many of these entertainment sites provide links to related shopping sites.

Many of the sites on the Internet are created for recreational rather than informational purposes. Commercial sites place key words in their titles to attract search engine hits and users. Additionally, commercial search engines make money by collecting advertising revenues. When

FIGURE 1.3 The *New York Times* website is an example of a news site.

©2001 The New York Times Company. Reprinted by permission.

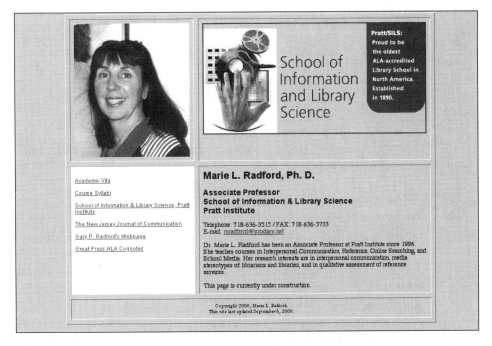

FIGURE 1.4 Marie L. Radford's site is an example of a personal website. She also uses tables to organize elements on the page (see Chapter 4).

Reprinted with permission from Marie L. Radford.

using the Web as an information source, you could end up with a mixture of many different types of sites.

Did you know that commercial sites (dotcoms) often pay search engines to have their sites retrieved first? Commercial sites (such as beer companies) that want to attract young men to their web pages also may include hot words such as *sex* on their sites so that surfers retrieve them when doing "extracurricular" research.

WHEN TO USE THE WEB FOR RESEARCH

Now that you know the essentials for using the Web for researching class assignments, let's look at the types of assignments you might have and when you should use the Web (see Table 1.3).

- Rather than operating with a knee-jerk reaction to reach for the mouse every time you have to look up a fact or write a paper, it is smart to know when web resources can help and when to go someplace else.
- As previously noted, your library home page can be a great starting point for entering into web research (Figure 1.5 on page 18). Table 1.3 has been provided to help you become more discriminating when using the Web.

SUMMARY

In this chapter you read about

- The rock-bottom basics of WWW searching, including
    Types of information found on the Web
    Some basic terminology
    Good news about searching the WWW for assignments
    Bad news about web searching and some words of caution
    Ten essentials for using the WWW for research

"It is shocking, but sometimes you just have to get dressed, leave the dorm room, and head for the library!"

TABLE 1.3   When to Use the Web for Assignments

ASSIGNMENT	USE THE WWW	USE ANOTHER RESOURCE
Find a fact.	Try the ready reference sites listed on p. 19.	Finding facts on the WWW is usually a time-consuming task. It is quicker to go to the library and look up facts. One site to try is Research-It! (www.iTools.com/research-it/research-it.html). This site searches many individual reference sources for facts.
Find a statistic.	Try the government, legal, statistical, U.S., and world resources found on p. 20.	Ditto! But you can find authoritative statistical sources on the Web such as the *Information Please Almanac* (www.infoplease.com) and FedStats (www.fedstats.gov). See pp. 19–21 for a list.
Build a reference list on a topic (using books and journal articles).	Books—Use your library's online catalog (i.e., what used to be a card catalog, remember?). Journals—Use journal indexes on your topic at your library home page.	

TABLE 1.3   (continued)

ASSIGNMENT	USE THE WWW	USE ANOTHER RESOURCE
Collect general background information for a research paper or oral report.	Use a search engine. The WWW can provide basic information on just about any topic. Caution! Don't accept information as fact from dotcoms. Verify using another source when possible.	Use library print resources, such as current encyclopedias.
Write a research paper or oral report using scholarly journals (refereed or juried).	Use journal indexes on your topic at your library home page. But it is nearly impossible to find full-text journal articles using a WWW search engine.	
Write a research paper or oral report using books.	Use your library online catalog, which contains all the books your library owns.	
Check book citations (or complete a partial citation).	Use your library online catalog. Use Amazon (www.amazon.com) or Barnes and Noble (www.bn.com).	
Research a current event.	Many free websites offer news. Caution! Make sure you are using an authoritative source such as the *New York Times* website (www.nytimes.com). See p. 21 for a list.	
Investigate a controversial topic.	Government sites offer easily accessible information on legislation, such as gun control bills. See Thomas (thomas.loc.gov), for example. Proceed with caution! Many websites on controversial topics are *largely* opinion, not fact.	
Gather general biographical information.	Some traditional print biographical resources, such as *Current Biography*, are now available online. Check with your library to see whether they subscribe.	Use library print resources. Any biographical information found through search engines should be verified.

(continued)

....

TABLE 1.3   (continued)

....

ASSIGNMENT	USE THE WWW	USE ANOTHER RESOURCE
Gather literary biographical information.	Check library home page to see whether your library has an online resource for this area (e.g., *GALE's Biography Resource Center*).	If your library home page does not have an online resource, go to the library and ask for help. Again, verify any information found through search engines.
Research books.		For most books you still have to go to the library. Exceptions include digitized books for which copyright has expired, for example "Bartleby" (www.bartleby. com) and electronic libraries of e-books, such as netLibrary if your library subscribes.
Present images, pictures, graphs, and tables.	Use a search engine. More and more graphics are available on the Web. Caution! You may not be able to download or print out to your satisfaction.	
Interpret a poem or passage.		You can find some literary criticism on the Web, but it is more easily found at the library.
Find a mathematical or chemical formula.		This information is difficult to find on the Web.
Find demographic information.	Most states have demographic information posted on their websites. Some data is outdated, so verify all dates. Also check government sites (see p. 20 for a list).	Some demographic data is very difficult to find on the Web and may require the help of a librarian.

••

TABLE 1.3 (continued)
••

ASSIGNMENT	USE THE WWW	USE ANOTHER RESOURCE
Obtain company information.	Subscription websites such as Hoovers.com and Lexis-Nexis have excellent information. However, they are not free services and your library must subscribe.	Caution! You can find some company information at company websites, but it is better to check the library.
Obtain legislative information.	The Library of Congress supports Thomas (thomas.loc.gov), a great site that provides current and authoritative information on legislation and laws.	
Obtain medical information.		Caution! Make sure you verify medical information found on the Web and are searching an authoritative site such as the American Cancer Society (www.cancer.org).
View maps.	Several good websites exist for maps (see p. 21 for a list). Caution! Some web maps may be out of date.	

- Different types of websites, including
    - Advocacy
    - Business
    - Information
    - News
    - Personal
    - Entertainment
- When to use the Web for assignments
    - Using your library's home page to find books, journal articles, and complete citation information

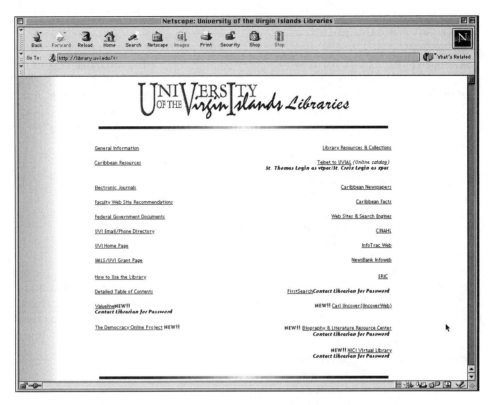

FIGURE 1.5   Some of the best information on the Web can be found by using your university library site.

Reprinted with permission from the Ralph M. Paiewonsky Library of the University of the Virgin Islands.

Using WWW search engines to find current events, images, pictures, graphs, tables, some demographic information, and general background information on most topics

Using print resources from the library to find facts, statistics, literary biographical information, and to verify information found on the Web.

You now have a good idea of the basics of using the Web for research. In the following chapters, your comfort level will rise as you discover more about the different types of websites, how to evaluate the content on sites, and how to deal with sticky ethical and copyright issues.

NOTHING BUT THE BEST
GREAT WEBSITES FOR RESEARCH

Ready Reference: Fact Finders, Dictionaries, and Encyclopedias

Bartlett's Familiar Quotations
www.bartleby.com

Encyclopedia Britannica (by subscription)
www.britannica.com

Information Please (also includes Sports
    Almanac, Entertainment Almanac,
    Columbia Encyclopedia, and
    Information Please Dictionary)
www.infoplease.com

Medical Dictionary
www.medterms.com

**Merriam-Webster's Collegiate Dictionary
    & Thesaurus**
www.m-w.com

Merck Manual of Diagnosis and Therapy
    (medical, diseases)
www.merck.com/pubs/mmanual

Old Farmer's Almanac
www.almanac.com

One Look Dictionaries
www.onelook.com

Research-It!
www.iTools.com/research-it

Roget's Thesaurus
www.thesaurus.com

Biographical Information

Lives, the Biography Resource
www.amillionlives.com

Biography.com
www.biography.com

Nobel Prize Winners
www.nobel.se

Saints and Angels
saints.catholic.org

Directories: People, Places, Addresses

Ameritech's Internet Yellow Pages
www.smartpages.com

AT&T Any Who
anywho.com

Bigfoot
bigfoot.com

City Search
citysearch.com

411.com
www.411.com

Infospace
www.infospace.com

WorldPages
www.worldpages.com

Switchboard
www.switchboard.com

Who Where
www.whowhere.com

Financial and Corporate Sources

Big Charts
www.bigcharts.com

CI: Corporate Information
www.corporateinformation.com

MSNBC
www.msnbc.com

Wall Street Journal
www.wsj.com

Yahoo Business News
dailynews.yahoo.com/h/bs

Government, Legal, Statistical, US and World Resources

American Memory (maps, journals,
  photos, sound, and video on
  U.S. history)
memory.loc.gov

Bureau of Labor Statistics
www.bls.gov

Country Studies/Area Handbook (covers
  92 countries)
lcweb2.loc.gov/frd/cs

**FedStats: One stop shopping for Federal
  Statistics**
www.fedstats.gov

Fifty States and Capitals
www.50states.com

Findlaw (directory of free legal and
  government resources)
www.findlaw.com

**Foreign Government Resources
  on the Web**
www.lib.umich.edu/libhome/
  Documents.center/foreign.html

Gallup Opinion Polls
www.gallup.com

GPO (U.S. Government Printing
  Office)
www.gpo.gov

InfoNation (information on 185 U.N.
  member countries)
www.un.org/Pubs/CyberSchoolBus/
  infonation/e_infonation.htm

IRS (tax publications and forms)
www.irs.gov/forms_pubs

Library of Congress
lcweb.loc.gov

Meta-Index for U.S. Legal Research
gsulaw.gsu.edu/metaindex

NASA
www.nasa.gov

NOLO (law for all)
www.nolo.com

NOLO Legal Encyclopedia
www.nolo.com/encyclopedia

Occupational Outlook Handbook
www.bls.gov/ocohome.htm

PAIS (Public Affairs Information Service)
www.pais.org

POTUS: Presidents of the U.S.
www.ipl.org/ref/POTUS

**Thomas—U.S. Congress on the
  Internet**
thomas.loc.gov

U.S. Postal Service
www.usps.com

World Fact Book (information produced by
  the CIA on 267 countries)
www.odci.gov/cia/publications/factbook

Zip Code Look-Up
www.usps.gov/ncsc

Maps

Perry-Castaneda Library Map Collection
    (2100 maps, not local maps)
www.lib.texas.edu/maps

MapQuest
www.mapquest.com

Topozone (topographical maps of the
    United States)
www.topozone.com

Museums

Exploratorium (science museum)
www.exploratorium.edu

Museum of Modern Art, NYC
www.moma.org

National Gallery of Art
www.nga.gov

News Sources

ABC
www.abcnews.com

Associated Press
wire.ap.org

CNN (Cable News Network)
www.cnn.com

CBS
www.cbs.com

CNET
www.news.com

ESPN (sports news)
www.espn.go.com

NewspaperLinks
www.newspaperlinks.com

Internet News
www.internetnews.com

Internet Week
www.internetweek.com

News 365 (links to 10,000 media sites)
www.news365.com

Newsforge
www.newsforge.com

New York Times
www.nytimes.com

Reuters
www.reuters.com

BIBLIOGRAPHY FOR FURTHER READING

Abbate, J. (1999). *Inventing the Internet.* Cambridge: The MIT Press.

Ackermann, Ernest C., & Hartman, Karen. (2000). *Information searcher's guide to searching and researching on the Internet and World Wide Web.* Wilsonville, OR: Franklin, Beedle, & Associates.

Alexander, Janet E., & Tate, Marsha Ann. (1999). *Web wisdom: How to evaluate and create information quality on the web.* Mahwah, NJ: Lawrence Erlbaum.

Andriot, Laurie. (2000). *Internet blue pages: The guide to federal government web sites, 2001–2002 Edition.* Medford, NJ: Information Today.

Bare Bones 101: A basic tutorial on searching the Web, www.sc.edu/beaufort/library/bones.html.

Basch, Reva, & Bates, Mary Ellen. (2000). *Researching online for dummies.* (2nd ed.). Foster City, CA: IDG Books Worldwide.

Berkman, Robert I. (2000). *Find it fast: How to uncover expert information on any subject online or in print.* New York: HarperResource.

Berners-Lee, T. (1999). *Weaving the Web.* San Francisco: HarperCollins.

Cailliau, Robert, & Gillies, James. (2000). *How the Web was born: The story of the World Wide Web.* New York: Oxford University Press.

Carbone, Nick. (2000). *Writing online: A student's guide to the Internet and World Wide Web.* New York: Houghton Mifflin.

Chamberlain, Ellen. (2001). *"Bare bones." A basic tutorial on searching the Web.* Available online at http://www.sc.edu/beaufort/library/bones.html.

Cohen, Laura B. (1999, August). The Web as a research tool: Teaching strategies for instructors. *CHOICE Supplement 3, 20–44.*

Doyle, Terrence A., & Gotthoffer, Doug. (2000). *Quick guide to the Internet for speech communication.* Boston: Allyn and Bacon.

Gralla, Preston, Ishida, Sarah, Reimer, Mina, & Adams, Steph. (1999). *How the Internet works, Millennium Edition.* Indianapolis: Que Education and Training.

Levine, John, Baroudi, Carol, & Young, Margaret. (2000). *The Internet for dummies.* Indianapolis: Que Education and Training.

Maloy, Timothy K. (1999). *The Internet research guide.* (2nd ed.). New York: Allworth Press.

Radford, Marie L., & Wagner, Kurt W. (2000). Communication webagogy 2.0: More click, less drag. *New Jersey Journal of Communication, 8*(2), 245–249.

Smith, Leroy Darland, & Satterwhite, Robin Rabun. (2000). *Debunking the Web: Evaluating Internet resources.* Littleton, CO: Libraries Unlimited.

Want, Robert S. (2000). *How to search the Web: A quick reference guide to finding things on the World Wide Web.* New York: Want Publishing.

• •

CHAPTER 2

Search Engines and Subject Directories

Your professor has just assigned you to give a five-minute speech on the topic of gun control. After a (hopefully brief) panic attack, you begin to think of what type of information you need to write the speech. To create an interesting introduction, you decide to involve your classmates by taking a straw poll of their views for and against gun control; next following this up by giving some statistics on how many people in the United States favor (or oppose) gun control legislation; and finally by outlining the arguments on both sides of the issue.

If you already know the correct URL for an authoritative website such as Gallup Opinion Polls (www.gallup.com) or other sites from Chapter 1, you are in great shape! However, what do you do when you don't have a clue as to which website has information on your topic? In these cases, many, many people routinely (and mistakenly) go to Yahoo! and type in a single term (e.g., *guns*). This approach is sure to bring first a smile to your face when the results offer you 200,874 hits on your topic, but just as quickly make you grind your teeth in frustration when you start scrolling down the hit list and find sites that range from gun dealerships, to reviews of the video *Young Guns,* to aging fan sites for Guns and Roses.

Finding information on a specific topic on the Web is a challenge. The more intricate your research need, the more difficult it is to find the one or two best websites that feature the quality information you want. This chapter is designed to help you avoid frustration and focus in on the right site for your research by using search engines, subject directories, and metasites.

SEARCH ENGINES

Search engines (sometimes called search services) are becoming more numerous on the Web (see Figure 2.1). Originally, they were designed to help users search the Web by topic. More recently, search engines have added features that enhance their usefulness, such as searching specific

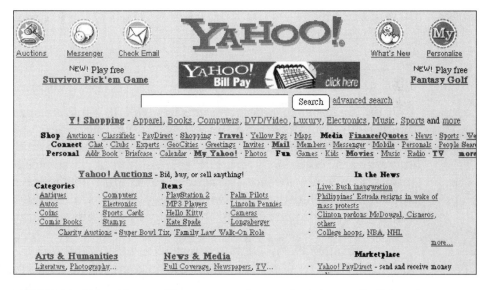

FIGURE 2.1   Yahoo! is one of the most popular search engines on the Internet.

material on the Web (e.g., only sites of educational institutions—dot.edu), retrieving just one site that the search engine touts as most relevant (e.g., Ask Jeeves, at www.aj.com), or retrieving up to 10 sites that the search engine ranks as most relevant (e.g., Google, at www.google.com).

According to Cohen (1999),

> A search engine service provides a searchable database of Internet files collected by a computer program called a wanderer, crawler, robot, worm, or spider. Indexing is created from the collected files, and the results are presented in a schematic order. There are no selection criteria for the collection of files.
>
> A search service therefore consists of three components: (1) a spider, a program that traverses the Web from link to link, identifying and reading pages; (2) an index, a database containing a copy of each Web page gathered by the spider; and (3) a search engine mechanism, software that enables users to query the index and then returns results in a schematic order. (p. 31)

One problem students often have in their use of search engines is that they are deceptively easy to use, like our search example of guns, no matter what is typed into the handy box at the top, links to numerous websites appear instantaneously, lulling students into a false sense of security. If so much was retrieved, surely *some* of it must be useful. *Wrong!* Many websites are very light on substantive content, which is not what you need for academic endeavors. Finding just the right website has been likened to finding diamonds in the desert.

As you can see by Cohen's definition, one reason for this is that most search engines use indexes developed by machines. Therefore they are indexing terms not concepts. The search engine cannot tell the difference between the keyword *crack* meaning a split in the sidewalk, and *crack* referring to the street drug crack cocaine. To use search engines properly takes some skill. This chapter provides tips to help you use search engines more effectively. First, however, take a look at the different types of search engines and examples in Table 2.1

 AltaVista has launched Raging Search (www.raging.com), which uses the same index as AltaVista, but no frills! An interesting return to a simpler approach, this search engine promises fast results without the extras.

"Talk about an information explosion! Now, in addition to <u>portals</u>, which offer a variety of services beyond mere search engines (such as customized shopping, news, weather, etc.), there are <u>vortals</u>, which have been described as 'portals on steroids'! Examples of university library portals are MyUW from the University of Washington (http://myuw.washington.edu) and MyUCLA from the University of California Los Angeles (http://www.my.ucla.edu)."

TABLE 2.1   Types of Search Engines

TYPE	DESCRIPTION	EXAMPLES
First Generation	Nonevaluative; does not evaluate results in terms of content or authority Returns results ranked by relevancy along with the number of times the term(s) entered appear, usually in the first paragraph or page of the site	**AltaVista** www.altavista.com **Excite** www.excite.com **HotBot** www.HotBot.com **Go.com** www.go.com **Lycos** www.lycos.com
Second Generation	More creative in displaying results Results ordered by characteristics such as concept, document type, website, and popularity, rather than relevancy	**Ask Jeeves** www.aj.com **Direct Hit** www.directhit.com **Google!** www.google.com **HotLinks** www.hotlinks.com **Simplifind** www.simpli.com **SurfWax** www.surfwax.com

TABLE 2.1   (continued)

TYPE	DESCRIPTION	EXAMPLES
Evaluative Search Engines		**About.Com** www.about.com
Commercial portals	Provide additional features such as customized news, stock quotations, weather reports, shopping, and so forth Meant to be used as a one stop web guide Profit from prominent advertisements and fees charged to featured sites	**GoNetwork** www.go.com **Google Web Directory** directory.google.com **LookSmart** www.looksmart.com **My Starting Point** www.stpt.com **NBCi** www.nbci.com **Open Directory Project** dmoz.org **Yahoo!** www.yahoo.com
Metasearch engines—integrated result	Display results for search engines in one list Remove duplicates Return only portions of results from each engine	**Beaucoup.com** www.beaucoup.com **Cyber411** www.cyber411.com **Mamma** www.mamma.com **MetaCrawler** www.metacrawler.com **Northern Light** www.nlsearch.com
Metasearch engines—non-integrated results	Comprehensive search Displays results from each search engine in separate results sets Duplicates remain You must sift through all sites	**Dogpile** www.dogpile.com **Global Federated Search** Jin.dis.vt.edu/fedsearch **GoHip** www.gohip.com **1Blink** www.1blink.com **ProFusion** www.profusion.com

QUICK TIPS FOR MORE EFFECTIVE USE OF SEARCH ENGINES

1. Use a search engine when
   - You have a narrow topic to search.
   - You want to search the full text of countless web pages.
   - You want to retrieve a large number of sites.
   - The features of the search engine (e.g., searching specific information on the Web) help with your search.
   - You are searching a complex topic with more than one concept or subject (e.g., the effect of television violence on children).
   - You want to use power search options.
   - You want to search for a phrase or series of words (e.g., "total solar eclipse").

2. Always use Boolean operators to combine terms. Searching a single term is a sure way to retrieve a very large number of web pages, few, if any, of which are on target.
   - Always check the search engine Help feature to find what symbols are used for the operators as these vary (e.g., some engines use the & or + symbol for *AND*).
   - Boolean operators include the words *AND*—to narrow the search and to make sure that *both* terms are included (e.g., children *AND* violence); *OR*—to broaden the search and to make sure that *either* term is included (e.g., child *OR* children *OR* juveniles); and *NOT*— to *exclude* one term (e.g., eclipse *NOT* lunar).
   - When using the Boolean operator *OR*, try to think of as many terms as possible that suit your topic (e.g., solar *OR* sun *OR* lunar *OR* moon *AND* eclipse) rather than just solar *AND* eclipse. This will improve your search results.

3. Use appropriate symbols to indicate important terms and to indicate phrases (see the Tip on page 29).

4. Use word stemming (i.e., truncation) to find all variations of a word. (Check the search engine Help for symbols.)
   - If you want to retrieve *child, child's,* or *children,* use *child**. (Some engines use other symbols, such as !, #, or $.)
   - Some engines automatically search singular and plural terms. (Check Help to see whether yours does.)

5. Because search engines only search a portion of the Web, use several search engines or a meta–search engine to extend your reach.

6. Remember, search engines are mostly mindless drones that do not evaluate. Do not rely on them to find the best websites on your topic. Use subject directories or metasites to ensure value.

....

The following strategies are your best bet for constructing a search according to Cohen (1999):

Use a plus sign (+) in front of terms you want to retrieve: +solar   +eclipse

Place a phrase in double quotation marks: "solar eclipse"

Combine the phrases   "+solar eclipse"   "+South America"

FINDING THOSE DIAMONDS IN THE DESERT: USING SUBJECT DIRECTORIES AND METASITES

Although some search engines, such as Magellan (magellan.excite.com), do evaluate the websites they index, most search engines do not make any judgment on the worth of the content. They just return a long, sometimes very long, list of sites that contained your keyword. However, human indexers, usually librarians or subject experts, have developed **subject directories,** which are defined by Cohen (1999) as follows:

> A subject directory is a service that offers a collection of links to Internet resources submitted by site creators or evaluators and organized into subject categories. Directory services use selection criteria for choosing links to include, though the selectivity varies among services. (p. 27)

World Wide Web subject directories are useful when you want to explore sites on your topic that have been reviewed, evaluated, and selected for their authority, accuracy, and value. (See Chapter 3 for an in-depth discussion of evaluation criteria.) They can be real time-savers for students because subject directories weed out the commercial, lightweight, or biased websites. Choose subject directories to ensure you are searching the highest-quality web pages. As an added bonus, subject directories periodically check weblinks to ensure fewer dead-end and out-dated links.

Metasites are similar to subject directories, but are more specific in nature, usually dealing with one scholarly field or discipline. Some examples of subject directories and metasites are found in Table 2.2 (see Figures 2.2 and 2.3 on page 33).

....

TABLE 2.2   Smart Searching: Subject Directories and Metasites
....

TYPE	EXAMPLES
General (covers many topics)	**Internet and Subject Resources** www2.lib.udel.edu/subj
	AlphaSearch (Hekman Digital Library, Calvin College) www.calvin.edu/library/searreso/internet/as
	Federal Web Locator www.infoctr.edu/fwl
	Galaxy galaxy.einet.net
	Needle in a Cyberstack, the InfoFinder members.home.net/albeej
	Infomine: Scholarly Internet Resource Collections infomine.ucr.edu
	InfoSurf: Resources by Subject www.library.ucsb.edu/subj
	Librarian's Index to the Internet www.lii.org
	Martindale's "The Reference Desk" www-sci.lib.uci.edu/~martindale/Ref.html
	PINAKES: A Subject Launchpad www.hw.ac.uk/libWWW/irn/pinakes/pinakes.html
	Refdesk www.refdesk.com
	Selected Reference Sites www.mnsfld.edu/depts/lib/mu-ref.html
	WWW Virtual Library www.vlib.org
Subject Oriented	
Communication Studies	**First Monday** (online journal) www.firstmonday.org **Journal of Computer-Mediated Communication** www.ascuse.org/jcmc **North American Data Communications Museum** www.nadcomm.com **University of Iowa Department of Communication Studies** www.uiowa.edu/~commstud/resources

TABLE 2.2　(continued)

TYPE	EXAMPLES
Subject Oriented *(continued)*	
Cultural Studies	**Resource Center for Cyberculture Studies** otal.umd.edu/~rccs
	Sara Zupko's Cultural Studies Center www.popcultures.com
Education	**Educational Virtual Library** www.csu.edu.au/education/library.html
	ERIC (Education Resources Information Center) ericir.sunsite.syr.edu
	Kathy Schrock's Guide for Educators school.discovery.com/schrockguide
Journalism	**Journalism Resources** bailiwick.lib.uiowa.edu/journalism
	Journalism and Media Criticism picard.montclair.edu/english/furr/media.html
Literature	**A Celebration of Women Writers** digital.library.upenn.edu/women
	Norton Web Source to American Literature www.wwnorton.com/naal
	Online Literary Criticism Collection (Internet Public Library) www.ipl.org/ref/litcrit
	Project Gutenberg (over 3,000 full text titles) www.gutenberg.net
	World Wide Words (History of English language and new word development) www.worldwidewords.org
E-books	**Alex Catalogue of Electronic Texts** www.infomotions.com/alex
	Banned Books Online digital.library.upenn.edu/books/banned-books.html
	Badosa www.badosa.com/

(continued)

TYPE	EXAMPLES
E-books *(continued)*	**The EServer** eserver.org
	Bibliomania www.bibliomania.com
	Humanities Text Initiative www.hti.umich.edu
	Free Ebook and Etext collections list publishing.about.com/arts/publishing/cs/etexts/ index.htm?terms=free+ebook
	NetLibrary www.netlibrary.com
	Perseus Digital Library www.perseus.tufts.edu
	Project Gutenberg www.gutenberg.org
	Bartleby.com www.bartleby.com
	Adobe Ebooks bookstore.glassbook.com/store/default.asp
	Amazon Ebooks www.amazon.com/exec/obidos/tg/browse/-/551440/ ref=b_tn_eb/102-0365954-4996159
	Bibliobytes www.bb.com/
	Ebook Library etext.virginia.edu/ebooks/
	Internet classics archive classics.mit.edu/index.html
	Inform-It Free Library www.informit.com/free_library/
Medicine & health	**PubMed** (National Library of Medicine's index to medical journals, 1966 to present) www.pubmed.gov
	RxList: The Internet Drug Index rxlist.com
	Go Ask Alice (health and sexuality) www.goaskalice.columbia.edu
Technology	CNET www.cnet.com

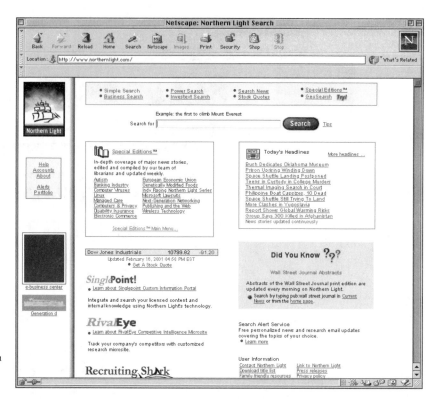

FIGURE 2.2
Northern Light is a meta–search engine with integrated results.

Reprinted with permission from Northern Light Technology, Inc. Copyright 2001.

FIGURE 2.3
Dogpile is an example of a meta–search engine with nonintegrated results.

Reprinted with express permission of InfoSpace, Inc. All rights reserved.

FIGURE 2.4   The William Paterson University library site is an outstanding example of a virtual library on the Internet.

Reprinted with permission.

Another closely related group of sites are the *virtual library* sites, sometimes called *digital library* sites (see Figure 2.4). Hopefully, your campus library has an outstanding website for both on-campus and off-campus access to resources. If not, you can access several virtual library sites that are listed in Table 2.3), although some of the resources are subscription based and accessible only to students of that particular university or college. These sites are useful because, like subject directories and metasites, experts have organized websites by topic and selected only those of highest quality.

SUMMARY

In this chapter you read about

- Types of search engines
    First generation—basic search engine
    Second generation—enhanced searching features
    Portals—offer a range of customized search and service features
    Meta–search engines—search multiple search engines

....

TABLE 2.3   Virtual Library Sites

....

Public Libraries

Internet Public Library	www.ipl.org
New York Public Library	www.nypl.org

University/College Libraries

Bucknell	www.library.bucknell.edu
Cas Western	www.cwru.edu/uclibraries.html
Dartmouth	www.dartmouth.edu/~library
Duke	www.lib.duke.edu
Franklin and Marshall	www.library.fandm.edu
Harvard	www.harvard.edu/museums
Penn State	www.libraries.psu.edu
Princeton	infoshare1.princeton.edu
Stanford	www.stanford.edu/home/libraries
ULCA	www.library.ucla.edu
William Paterson University	www.wpunj.edu/library
University of the Virgin Islands	library.uvi.edu

Special Library

Library of Congress	lcweb.loc.gov

Integrated results—displays results in one list with duplicates removed

Nonintegrated results—comprehensive search that displays results in separate sets with duplicates remaining

- Subject directories and metasites

    People

    Places

    Addresses

You now know how to search for information and use search engines more effectively. In the next two chapters, you learn more tips for evaluating the information that you find and for citing it properly.

BIBLIOGRAPHY FOR FURTHER READING
••

Ackermann, Ernest, & Hartman, Karen. (2001). *The information seeker's guide to searching and researching on the Internet and World Wide Web.* (2nd ed.). Wilsonville, OR: Franklin, Beedle, & Associates.

Berkman, Robert I. (2000). *Find it fast: How to uncover expert information on any subject online or in print.* New York: HarperResource.

Cohen, Laura B. (2000, August). Searching the Web: The human element emerges. *CHOICE Supplement 37,* 17–31.

Glossbrenner, Alfred, & Glossbrenner, Emily. (1999). *Search engines for the World Wide Web.* (2nd ed.). Berkeley, CA: Peachpit Press.

Hock, Randolph. (1999). *The extreme searchers guide to Web search engines: A handbook for the serious searcher.* Medford, NJ: CyberAge Books.

Holscher, Christoph, & Strube, Gerhard. (2000, June). Web search behavior of Internet experts and newbies. *Computer Networks, 33*(1), 337–346.

Introna, Lucas D., & Nissenbaum, Helen. (2000). Shaping the web: Why the politics of search engines matters. *The Information Society, 16*(3), 169–185.

Ketchell, Debra S. (2000, December). Too many channels: Making sense out of portals and personalization. *Information Technology and Libraries, 19*(4), 175–179.

Lakos, Amos, & Gray, Chris. (2000, December). Personalized library portals as an organizational culture change agent. *Information Technology and Libraries, 19*(4), 169–174.

Miller, Michael. (2000). *Complete idiot's guide to Yahoo!* Indianapolis, IN: Que.

Miller, Michael. (2000). *Complete idiot's guide to online search secrets.* Indianapolis, IN: Que.

Paul, Nora, Williams, Margot, & Hane, Paula. (1999). *Great scouts!: CyberGuides for subject searching on the Web.* Medford, NJ: Information Today.

Sherman, Chris, & Price, Gary. (2001). *The invisible Web: Uncovering information sources search engines can't see.* Medford, NJ: Information Today.

CHAPTER 3

Content Evaluation

Bingo! You've hit the jackpot! You've found a great website. Now what? The website you are viewing on your monitor seems like *the* perfect website for your research. But, are you sure? Why is it perfect? What criteria are you using to determine whether this website suits your purpose?

Think about it. Where on earth can anyone "publish" information regardless of the accuracy, currency, or reliability of the information? The Internet has opened up a world of opportunity for posting and distributing information and ideas to virtually everyone, even those who might post bogus information for fun, or those with ulterior motives for promoting their point of view. Armed with the guidelines provided in this chapter, you can dig through the vast amount of useless information on the World Wide Web to uncover the valuable information. Because practically anyone can post and distribute their ideas on the Web, you need to develop a new set of critical thinking skills that focus on the evaluation and quality of information, rather than be influenced and manipulated by slick graphics and flashy moving java scripts.

Way back before the existence of online sources, the validity and accuracy of a source was more easily determined. For example, when a book gets to the publishing stage, it has gone through many critiques, validation of facts, reviews, editorial changes, and so forth. Furthermore, ownership is clear because the author's name is attached to it. The publisher's reputation is on the line too. If the book turns out to have bogus information, reputations and money can be lost. In addition, books available in your university library are further reviewed by professional librarians and selected for library purchase because of their accuracy and value to students. Journal articles downloaded or printed from online subscription services, such as Infotrac, ProQuest, EbscoHost, or other full-text databases, are put through the same scrutiny as the paper versions of the journals.

On the World Wide Web, however, Internet service providers (ISPs) simply give website authors a place to store information. The website author can post information that may not be validated or tested for accuracy. One mistake students typically make is to assume that all information on the Web is of equal value. Also, in the rush to get assignments in on time, students may not take the extra time to make sure that the information they are citing is accurate. It is easy to just cut and paste without really thinking about the content in a critical way. However, to make sure you are gathering accurate information and to get the best grade on your assignments, it is vital that you develop your critical ability to sift through the dirt to find those diamond nuggets.

WEB EVALUATION CRITERIA

So, here you are, at this potentially great site. Let's go through some ways you can determine if this site is one you can cite with confidence in your research. Keep in mind, ease of use is an issue, but learning how to determine the validity of data, facts, and statements is worthy of your time. The five traditional ways to check a paper source can also be applied to your web source: accuracy, authority, objectivity, coverage, and currency.

Accuracy

"When in doubt, leave the information out."

As described in Chapter 1, Internet searches are not the same as searches of library databases because much of the information on the Web has not been edited whereas information in databases has. It is your responsibility to make sure that the information you use in a school project is accurate. When you examine the content on a website or web page, you can ask yourself a number of questions to determine whether the information is accurate.

1. Is the information reliable?

2. Do the facts from your other research contradict the facts you find on this web page?

3. Do any misspellings and/or grammar mistakes indicate a hastily put-together website that has not been checked for accuracy?

4. Is the content on the page verifiable through some other source? Can you find similar facts elsewhere (journals, books, or other online sources) to support the facts you see on this web page?

5. Do you find links to other websites on a similar topic? If so, check those links to ascertain whether they back up the information you see on the web page you are interested in using.

6. Is a bibliography of additional sources for research provided? Lack of a bibliography doesn't mean the page isn't accurate, but having one allows you further investigation points to check the information.

7. Does the site of a research document or study explain how the data was collected and the type of research method used to interpret the data?

If you've found a site with information that seems too good to be true, it may be. You need to verify information that you read on the Web by cross-checking against other sources.

Authority

An important question to ask when you are evaluating a website is, Who is the author of the information? Do you know whether the author is a recognized authority in his or her field? Biographical information, references to publications, degrees, qualifications, and organizational affiliations can help to indicate an author's authority. For example, if you are researching the topic of laser surgery, citing a medical doctor would be better than citing a college student who has had laser surgery.

The organization sponsoring the site can also provide clues about whether the information is fact or opinion. Examine how the information was gathered and the research method used to prepare the study or report. Other questions to ask include

1. Who is responsible for the content of the page? Although a webmaster's name is often listed, this person is not necessarily responsible for the content.
2. Is the author recognized in the subject area? Does this person cite any other publications he or she has authored?
3. Does the author list his or her background or credentials (e.g., Ph.D. degree, title such as professor, or other honorary or social distinction)?
4. Is there a way to contact the author? Does the author provide a phone number or email address?
5. If the page is mounted by an organization, is it a known, reputable one?
6. How long has the organization been in existence?
7. Does the URL for the web page end in the extension .edu or .org? Such extensions indicate authority, compared to dotcoms (.com), which are commercial enterprises. (For example, www.cancer.com takes you to an online drugstore that has a cancer information page; www.cancer.org is the American Cancer Society website.)

Ask yourself whether the author or organization presenting the information on the Web is an authority on the subject. If the answer is no, this may not be a good source of information.

Objectivity

Every author has a point of view, and some views are more controversial than others. Journalists try to be objective by providing both sides of a story. Academics attempt to persuade readers by presenting a logical argument, which cites other scholars' work. You need to look for two-sided arguments in news and information sites. For academic papers, you need to determine how the paper fits within its discipline and whether the author is using controversial methods for reporting a conclusion.

Authoritative authors situate their work within a larger discipline. This background helps readers evaluate the author's knowledge on a particular subject. You should ascertain whether the author's approach is controversial and whether he or she acknowledges this. More important, is the information being presented as fact or opinion? Authors who argue for their position provide readers with other sources that support their arguments. If no sources are cited, the material may be an opinion piece rather than an objective presentation of information. The following questions can help you determine objectivity:

1. Is the purpose of the site clearly stated, either by the author or the organization authoring the site?
2. Does the site give a balanced viewpoint or present only one side?
3. Is the information directed toward a specific group of viewers?
4. Does the site contain advertising?
5. Does the copyright belong to a person or an organization?
6. Do you see anything to indicate who is funding the site?

 ···

Everyone has a point of view. This is important to remember when you are using web resources. A question to keep asking yourself is, What is the bias or point of view being expressed here?

Coverage

Coverage deals with the breadth and depth of information presented on a website. Stated another way, it is about how much information is presented and how detailed the information is. Looking at the site map or index can give you an idea about how much information is contained on a site. This isn't necessarily bad. Coverage is a criteria that is tied closely to *your* research requirement. For one assignment, a given website may be too general for your needs. For another assignment, that same site might be perfect. Some sites contain very little actual information because pages are filled with links to other sites. Coverage also relates to objectivity. You should ask the following questions about coverage:

"Don't be impressed by Web Page Awards. The joke going around the Web is, there are so many different awards that every web page has at least one."

1. Does the author present both sides of the story, or is a piece of the story missing?

2. Is the information comprehensive enough for your needs?

3. Does the site cover too much, too generally?

4. Do you need more specific information than the site can provide?

5. Does the site have an objective approach?

In addition to examining what is covered on a website, equally revealing is what is not covered. Missing information can reveal a bias in the material. Keep in mind that you are evaluating the information on a website for your research requirements.

Currency

Currency questions deal with the timeliness of information. However, currency is more important for some topics than for others. For example, currency is essential when you are looking for technology-related topics and current events. In contrast, currency may not be relevant when you are doing research on Plato or Ancient Greece. In terms of websites, currency also pertains to whether the site is being kept up to date and links are being maintained. Sites on the Web are sometimes abandoned by their owners. When people move or change jobs, they may neglect to remove their site from the company or university server. To test currency, ask the following questions:

1. Does the site indicate when the content was created?

2. Does the site contain a last revised date? How old is the date? (In the early part of 2001, a university website gave a last updated date of 1901! This date was obviously a Y2K problem, but it does point out the need to be observant of such things!)

3. Does the author state how often he or she revises the information? Some sites are on a monthly update cycle (e.g., a government statistics page).

4. Can you tell specifically what content was revised?

5. Is the information still useful for your topic? Even if the last update is old, the site might still be worthy of use *if* the content is still valid for your research.

RELEVANCY TO YOUR RESEARCH: PRIMARY VERSUS SECONDARY SOURCES

Some research assignments require the use of primary (original) sources. Materials such as raw data, diaries, letters, manuscripts, and original accounts of events can be considered primary material. In most cases, these historical documents are no longer copyrighted. The Web is a great source for this type of resource.

Information that has been analyzed and previously interpreted is considered a secondary source. Sometimes secondary sources are more appropriate than primary sources. If, for example, you are asked to analyze a topic or to find an analysis of a topic, a secondary source of an analysis would be most appropriate. Ask yourself the following questions to determine whether the website is relevant to your research:

1. Is it a primary or secondary source?

2. Do you need a primary source?

3. Does the assignment require you to cite different types of sources? For example, are you supposed to use at least one book, one journal article, and one web page?

HELP IN EVALUATING WEBSITES

As described in Chapter 1, one shortcut to finding high-quality websites is using subject directories and metasites, which select the websites they index by similar evaluation criteria to those just described. If you want to learn more about evaluating websites, many colleges and universities provide sites that help you evaluate web resources (see Figure 3.1). The following list contains some excellent examples of these evaluation sites:

- Evaluating Quality on the Net—Hope Tillman, Babson College www.tiac.net/users/hope/findqual.html
- Critical Web Evaluation—Kurt W. Wagner, William Paterson University of New Jersey   euphrates.wpunj.edu/faculty/wagnerk
- Evaluation Criteria—Susan Beck, New Mexico State University lib.nmsu.edu/instruction/evalcrit.html

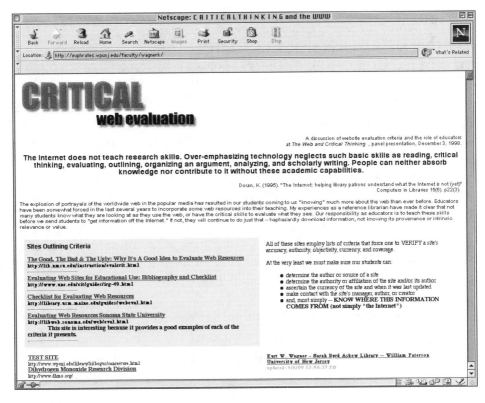

FIGURE 3.1   An example of a web evaluation site.

Reprinted with permission from Kurt W. Wagner.

A comparison of the criteria used by several noted web evaluation sites can be found in Table 3.1. Many books also contain information on web evaluation and on how the Web is being used unscrupulously. These books may point out what sites to stay away from. See the Bibliography for Further Reading at the end of Chapter 1 for a list of such books.

TABLE 3.1   Comparison of Web Evaluation Sites

WEBSITE AND URL	SOURCE	CRITERIA
About StudyWEB www.studyweb.com/about/ ratings.htm	American Computer Resources, Inc. (sells computers, mostly IBMs)	Visual content, reading level, "quality" (not defined)
Critical Thinking in an Online World www.library.ucsb.edu/untangle/ jones/html	University of California, Santa Barbara Library (Cabrillo College Internet librarian)	Fact vs. opinion, examine assumptions, be flexible and open-minded, be aware of ambiguity, look for reputable sources, focus on whole picture
Educom Review: Information www.educause.edu/pub/er/review/ reviewArticles/31231.html	EDUCAUSE Literacy as a Liberal Art (an organization focusing on information technology and education)	—
Evaluating Information Found on the Internet MiltonsWeb.mse.jhu.edu/ research/education/net.html	Johns Hopkins University Library	Author, publishing body, academic credibility, currency
Evaluating Internet Information medstate.med.utah.edu/resource/ doh/infoeval.html	University of Utah Library	Author, publisher/ sponsor, credibility bias/purpose, currency, site organization
Evaluating Web Sites www.lehigh.edu/~inref/guides/ evaluating.web.html	Lehigh University	Credibility, documentation, author, publisher, currency

(continued)

TABLE 3.1   (continued)

WEBSITE AND URL	SOURCE	CRITERIA
Evaluating World Wide Web Information webct.cc.purdue.edu:8900/web-ct/ courses/LIB101/evalSrcs/ evalweb.html	Purdue University Library	Author, link to local home page, institution, date of evaluation creation/revision, intended audience, purpose
Evaluating Web Resources www.delta.edu/~mkhiatt/ evaluating.html	Delta College (English teacher)	Author, publisher, credibility, agenda/ purpose/bias, documentation, currency
ICONnect: Curriculum Connections Overview www.ala.org/ICONN/evaluate. html	American Library Association's technology education initiative	Author/credibility; content, design and technical features; navigation; curriculum; connections; learning environment
Internet Source Validation Project www.stemnet.nf.ca/Curriculum/ Validate/validate.html	Memorial University (faculty of Education)	Accuracy, relevance, bias, credibility, author, publisher, documentation, currency, purpose/intent
Kathy Schrock's ABC's of Web Site Evaluation www.kathyschrock.net/abceval/	Author's website	Authorship, currency, spelling accuracy, credibility, relevance, bias, publisher
Kids Pick the Best of the Web "Top 10" Announced www.ala.org/news/topkidpicks. html	American Library Association (underwritten by Microsoft)	Level of fun and learning
Resource Selection and Information Evaluation alexia.lis.uiuc.edu/~janicke/ Evaluate.html	University of Illinois, Urbana-Champaign (Illinois State University librarian)	Format, scope, relation to other works, authority, treatment, arrangement, cost
Testing the Surf: Criteria for Evaluating Internet Information Sources info.lib.uh.edu/pr/v8/n3/ smit8n3.html	University of Houston	Accuracy, authority, currency, grammar, purpose and audience

••

TABLE 3.1   (continued)

••

WEBSITE AND URL	SOURCE	CRITERIA
Evaluating Web Resources muse.widener.edu/Wolfram-Memorial-Library/ webevaluation/webeval.htm	Widener University Library	Accuracy, authority, objectivity, currency, coverage
UCLA College Library Instruction: Thinking Critically about World Wide Web Resources www.library.ucla.edu/ libraries/college/help/critical/	UCLA Library	Audience, purpose, accuracy, author/producer, credibility, publisher, bias, graphical clarity
UG OOL: Judging Quality on the Internet www.open.uoguelph.ca/resources/ skills/judging.html	University of Guelph Ontario, Canada	Generation of source, validity, credibility, audience and purpose, currency, bias, documentation
Web Evaluation: Criteria lib.nmsu.edu/instruction/ evalcrit.html	New Mexico State University Library	Accuracy, author, bias/objectivity, currency, coverage
Web Page Credibility Checklist www.park.pvt.k12.md.us/ academics/research/ credcheck.htm	Park School of Baltimore	Currency, relevancy, accuracy, clarity, documentation

 •••
Using your common sense can also help you evaluate websites. For example, spelling mistakes and poor grammar indicate that a site has not been carefully checked for accuracy.

ADDITIONAL CRITERIA FOR EVALUATING WEBSITES
•••

A number of web evaluation sites add additional criteria for evaluating sites. Table 3.2 is an analysis of all the different criteria various librarians and professors recommend on their websites that pertain to evaluation measures. Seventeen websites created to evaluate the Web were reviewed.

TABLE 3.2   Rank of Additional Criteria for Evaluating Websites

CRITERIA	IMPORTANCE OF CRITERIA
Bias/purpose/objectivity	17
Currency	13
Author	12
Publisher	12
Credibility	10
Accuracy	10
Documentation	6
Relevance to user	5
Scope/coverage	4
Author's authority	4
Aesthetics/visual content	4
Authority	3
Intended audience	3
Clarity	3
Appropriateness of format	2
Navigation	2
Site access and usability	2
Validity	2
Learning environment	2
Information structure and design	2
Academic credibility	1
Content design and technical features	1
Date of creation	1
Link to local home page	1
Quality of links	1
Reading level	1
Relation to other works	1
Spelling	1

These sites identified the criteria listed in Table 3.2 as being important in site evaluation. In addition to the eight traditional criteria discussed in this chapter, spelling, grammar, navigation, and visual design elements were also identified as being important.

These additional criteria incorporate concepts that are presented in the next chapter, Chapter 4, "Visual Evaluation." You need to think critically, both visually and verbally, when evaluating websites. Because websites are designed as multimedia hypertexts, nonlinear texts, visual elements, and navigational tools are added to the evaluation process.

SUMMARY

In this chapter you read about

- Evaluating websites using five criteria to judge website content:
    Accuracy—How reliable is the information?
    Authority—Who is the author and what are his or her credentials?
    Objectivity—Does the website present a balanced or biased point of view?
    Coverage—Is the information comprehensive enough for your needs?
    Currency—Is the website up to date?
- Using additional criteria to judge website content, including publisher, documentation, relevance, scope, audience, appropriateness of format, and navigation
- Judging whether the site is made up of primary (original) or secondary (interpretive) sources
- Determining whether the information is relevant to your research
- Where to go for additional help in evaluating websites
- The best evaluation websites and the criteria they use

CRITICAL EVALUATION WEBSITES

Study Web
www.studyweb.com/about/ratings.htm

Critical Thinking in an Online World
www.library.ucsb.edu/untangle/jones.html

**Milton's Web: Evaluating Information
Found on the Internet**
MiltonsWeb.mse.jhu.edu/research/
education/net.html

Evaluating Scholarly/Information Sites on the Web
www.lehigh.edu/~inref/guides/evaluating.web.html

ICONnect
www.ala.org/ICONN/overview.html

Internet Source Validation Project
www.stemnet.nf.ca/Curriculum/Validate/validate.html

Kathy Schrock's the ABC's of Web Evaluation
www.kathyschrock.net/abceval/

Kids Pick the Best of the Web
www.ala.org/news/topkidpicks.html

Resource Selection and Information Evaluation
alexia.lis.uiuc.edu/~janicke/Evaluate.html

Testing the Surf: Criteria for Evaluating Internet Information Resources
info.lib.uh.edu/pr/v8/n3/smit8n3.html

Selecting the Right Source
www.library.ucla.edu/libraries/college/help/selectsource/

Judging Quality on the Net
www.open.uoguelph.ca/resources/skills/judging.html

Evaluation Criteria, Susan Beck
lib.nmsu.edu/instruction/evalcrit.html

Critical Web Evaluation
euphrates.wpunj.edu/faculty/wagnerk

Ten C's for Evaluating Web Sites
www.uwec.edu/Admin/Library/Guides/tencs.html

BIBLIOGRAPHY FOR FURTHER READING

Basch, Reva, & Bates, Mary Ellen. (2000). *Researching online for dummies.* (2nd ed.). Indianapolis: Hungryminds.

Bopp, R. E., & Smith, L. C. (Eds.). (2001). *Reference and information services: An introduction.* (3rd ed.). Englewood, CO: Libraries Unlimited.

Cooke, Alison. (1999). *Neal Schuman authoritative guide to evaluating information on the Internet.* New York: Neal Schuman.

Goldsborough, Reid. (2001, January–February). How to find the best Web sites. *Link-UP, 18*(1), 17.

Spyridakis, Jan H. (2000, August). Guidelines for authoring comprehensible Web pages and evaluating their success. *Technical Communication, 47*(3), 359–382.

Williams, Thomas R. (2000, August). Guidelines for designing and evaluating the display of information on the Web. *Technical Communication, 47*(3), 383–397.

CHAPTER 4

Visual
Evaluation

The ARPAnet, the original Internet, was developed to connect universities working on government projects. Gradually, a series of networks developed in the United States, including Usenet and BITNET, to connect more colleges. Eventually, all these various networks became interconnected and the Internet was born. The not-very-exciting black-and-white text orientation and serious nature of the early Internet made it unattractive to commercial interests. However, once the World Wide Web added point-and-click visual interfaces and graphics with video and audio capability, the Internet began to resemble familiar mass media, such as television and newspapers. As a result, the context of the Internet began to change; visually distinguishing between serious, academic, and commercial online information became much more difficult.

Currently, there is no gatekeeping or editorial review of information on the Internet. Almost anyone can design websites to express a point of view, whether positive or negative, good or bad. For example, serious concern is being raised about the growing number of hate speech sites on the Internet. Hate speech spreads racial bigotry, Holocaust denial, gay bashing, and other offensive and, sadly, sometimes deadly points of view, such as those of the white supremacist groups Aryan Nations, the Ku Klux Klan, and Resistance Records, a white-power record company. Some hate sites are professionally designed and contain strong visual logo elements that reflect the opinions expressed in the site. In addition to identifying websites with strongly biased content, savvy students also know how to recognize the visual manipulation techniques used by commercial web designers to capture your attention and distract you from a productive information search.

ADVERTISING ON THE WEB

Advertising is an integral part of mass media in the United States. It is through the revenues of advertising dollars that broadcast media survive to bring you popular programs such as *Survivor* or *Who Wants to Be a Millionaire?* Similarly, newspapers and magazines sell space to advertisers to help offset publishing costs. As the Web grew, it was made more attractive by graphical interfaces, and became present in more homes and businesses. The Web's graphic capabilities also attracted advertising and commercial sponsors. In the early days of radio and television, individual sponsors paid for the programming and in exchange they received air time to promote their products. Moreover, sponsoring a popular program helped create a positive image for the corporation. Today, companies such as Microsoft help sponsor educational sites on the Web. Sites with corporate sponsors generally feature a link to the sponsor's website.

One difference between traditional TV or radio commercials and Web advertising is that in the past, the viewer or listener did not have to do anything to see or hear the ads. Web advertising is different because you have to type in the URL (or click on a pop-up ad) to visit a commercial website. Web companies have developed many (mostly annoying!) strategies, including **push technology,** for getting the unsuspecting web surfer to visit their sites. An input device, the Cue Cat, which reads URL "bar codes" with one swipe, has been given away by the millions to make it easier for you to visit commercial sites.

Commercial activity on the Web can be placed into six categories: online storefront, Internet presence, content, mall, incentive site, and search engine. You may be surprised to see search engines listed as a commercial category in Chapter 1, but it is difficult not to notice the intrusive ads that are popping up on most web search engines, ads which are actually commercial sites that sell advertising space. For example, Yahoo! has an arrangement with Amazon.com to provide links to the Amazon site to purchase books.

Chapter 1 described a variety of different types of websites. Online storefronts enable people to purchase products directly through the Internet. In contrast, Internet presence sites provide a virtual presence for companies. Content sites are both free and fee based. Fee-based sites enable users to purchase information. For example, the *New York Times* (www. nytimes.com) provides free access to recent issues but charges users to download back-file articles for a fee of about $2.50. Other sponsored content sites, such as CNN (www.CNN.com) and *ADWEEK* (www. adweek.com), provide free online content to users. Malls are collections of online storefronts. Incentive sites pull users to the site by offering a contest, prize, or reason why people should access the site. These sites are created to help marketers generate traffic on their site. For example, Iwon.com is a search engine that gives away money as a way to increase its Internet traffic and Hotmail offers free email addresses. Search engines are often advertiser sponsored. See Chapter 2 for a list of the best ones to use.

VISUAL PRESENTATION

Creating web-based presentations requires authors to think about how to present information in a way that is both visually engaging and interactive. **Graphical user interfaces** enable computer users to interact with both visual and text-based icons, and hypertext enables web authors to connect web pages interactively. Today, students can easily add pictures and graphics to their word-processed assignments. But few students have been taught visual literacy skills used to create effective visual presentations. Consequently, students can become side-tracked by fancy graphics, animations, and the visual look of a website.

We live in a world full of visual media—television, newspapers, magazines, and billboards—filled with messages that fight for our attention. Designers use numerous visual techniques to capture our interest. These techniques include layout, color, movement, typography, and metaphor. Laying out art and copy on a page is a visual skill. The task is to place a variety of elements into an eye-catching and unified relationship. Some aesthetic principles from the fine arts, such as balance, contrast, and proportion, apply to web design.

To create balanced layouts, designers often place visual and verbal elements on a grid (see Figure 4.1). The grid provides a framework for a wide variety of different designs because placing images on several modular units and leaving other modules white creates contrast. In web design, a grid structure can be developed using table features. Visual and verbal information can be arranged in tables to create a balanced look for web pages (Figure 4.2). According to Dondis (1973), balance has important psychological and physical influences on human perception. To the receiver of visual information, the lack of balance and regularity is a disorienting factor. Therefore, information is better received when it is placed in a balanced layout.

FIGURE 4.1   Many designers use a basic grid system to organize elements on a page. Pictures, text, and graphics are placed in different areas of the grid to create a balanced layout.

USING TABLES TO ORGANIZE A WEB PAGE

text can also be placed inside a table
and arranged with images

FIGURE 4.2   When creating web pages, tables can be used to arrange visual and verbal elements into a gridlike layout. Marie L. Radford's personal home page also uses this technique.

Color

Colors also convey meaning that reinforce verbal messages. Warm colors—red, yellow, and orange—attract more attention than cool colors—blue, green, and purple. In addition to having different levels of attraction, colors also convey cultural meanings. Jan V. While (1990) describes an example in the following passage:

> Innumerable surveys have been made, and studying and understanding reaction to color is an important science, because purveyors of goods and services rely on these reactions to succeed in the marketplace. There are some useful pointers, for instance:
>
> Sugar is never packaged in green, because green carries connotations of sourness. It is packaged in blue, because blue is a color we associate with sweetness. (p. 22)

The implied meaning associated with colors can also help communicate an idea. For example, in web design, black is the normal default color for text and blue text usually indicates a hypertext link. By clicking on the blue type, another page is accessed. After selecting a blue text link, the color of the text changes to purple to indicate that the link has already been chosen.

The colors a web designer uses can help to set a tone for the page. When viewing a website, check to see whether the colors support the verbal information being presented. For instance, does the site use basic default colors (blue and black text with a grey background) to present basic information? If the site features green, does it discuss nature, money, financial issues, or gardening tips? If the site uses a black background with reversed white type, is it presenting a serious topic or issue? If the colors and the message conflict, the site can seem less credible.

Remember the saying, "You can't judge a book by its cover"? The same holds true for websites. You can't always judge the quality of information on a site by its graphics alone.

Don't Judge a Website by Its Production Values

The Web is a visual medium and judging websites also requires you to be visually alert. Professional designers know how to direct your attention toward graphic elements and how to create the illusion of credibility. However, great-looking websites may not be the best source of information. In contrast to traditional mass media with professional writers and editors, just about anyone can create a website and make it available on the network. Many sites, such as virtual libraries, are not designed by professional graphic artists. Instead librarians create virtual library sites. Virtual library sites, such as the Internet Public Library (www.ipl.org), may have low visual appeal, but the information they contain is highly valuable.

Similarly, the use of online visual and verbal metaphors can be confusing. For example, both academic institutions and commercial companies use the virtual library metaphor. The metaphor of a library online obviously parallels visiting one and most of our physical libraries are nonprofit or educational establishments. However, unlike physical libraries, some virtual ones are being set up by corporations and commercial companies. Don't assume that all the information you access through a virtual library is legitimate. Some of these sites have been established with the purpose of distributing a specific type of information; all points of view may not be represented. Moreover, the information accessible on a commercial virtual library site could reflect a bias of the company that supports it. An example is a virtual library site that provides computer information for commercial purposes, such as the Virtual Library of WWW Development (WWW.Stars.com/Vlib/).

Developing Visual Savvy

Being visually aware requires you to identify the **visual hierarchy** of a website, which is a group of visual (and verbal) elements arranged according to emphasis. Emphasis is achieved with contrast, stressing the relative importance, separation, or connection of graphic elements (see Figure 4.3 on page 58). Visual hierarchies are created to enhance the overall purpose of the message being communicated. For example, to create a visual hierarchy on a business website, the designer must decide which component is the most important, is less important, and is the least important. The purpose of a visual hierarchy is to focus the eye on the most important component of the message being communicated.

As previously stated, colors can be used both to reinforce a verbal message and to divert our attention. Contrast between colors on a page both draws attention to page elements and enhances readability. According to web designer Roger Black, in order of importance, the first color is white, the second color is black, and the third color is red. White is the best background color because black holds the highest contrast to white. The contrast between black and white makes pages easier to read. For example, web designers who are concerned with legibility issues avoid problematic color choices, such as putting yellow type on orange backgrounds, because not enough contrast exists between the type and the background to read the text easily. After white and black, the next important color is red. Red is nature's danger color; it attracts our attention. Roger Black (1997) says, "Red is perfect. Red headlines sell magazines on newsstands twice as much as any other color" (p. 36).

In addition to visual hierarchies and color, animation also attracts our attention. When designers place moving images on a page, they automatically grab our attention. It comes as no surprise that web advertisers are

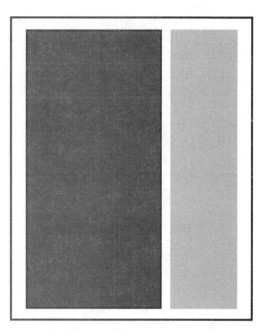

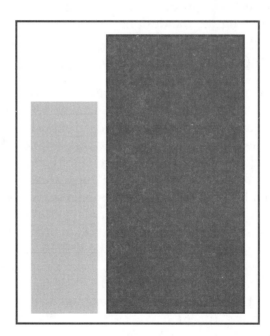

FIGURE 4.3   These three layouts are based on the same grid format. Notice how areas in the different layouts attract your attention to create visual hierarchies.

aware of the impact of movement on a web page, and many advertising banners are deliberately designed to pull our attention away from the content of a site. Clicking on the banner takes you to another page of advertising that is specifically designed to persuade you to purchase a product or service.

Graphics and Visual Interest

Text, images, and color can set a mood or tone for a website. For example, sites using the default colors of black type, blue links, and grey or white backgrounds imply a basic look or the idea of plain information. People who want to make information available on the Web and are not concerned about graphics might want to use this basic approach. Moreover, a fancy, colorful site that attracts your attention might be full of advertising and contain very little useful information.

Given the option of going to a website that is predominantly text based or one that is filled with graphics and video, most students choose the latter. However, sites with movie clips and sound clips are generally promotional sites that do not provide any serious information because they are designed to sell a media product. Moving graphics are generally not used by reference and digital library sites. Three reasons explain why. First, digital video takes a long time to download to a computer screen. Second, video images take up a tremendous amount of space or bandwidth, which makes them slow memory hogs. Finally, animations can detract students away from the important textual information located on the site.

Sites that contain scholarly information are often text oriented; their designers use graphics cautiously. An exception to this rule is educational medical and scientific sites that include visual simulations to explain complex concepts. Some of these sites use graphics effectively both to capture attention and to communicate ideas.

VISUAL EVALUATION OF WEBSITES

Today the Internet is filled with graphics and advertising that can distract the student from his or her research. Although many of us tune out commercials on television, the same is not always true about commercialism on the Web. The following are some graphic questions that you should consider when evaluating the presentation of websites:

1. Is the graphic designed to capture your attention?
2. Is the image being used as a form of visual persuasion to make you think or feel a certain way?
3. What type of emotional message does it convey?
4. Does the image complement and support the text?
5. Does the site use a visual metaphor and does it support the content?

Commercial Manipulation Strategies

The visual manipulation strategies used in commercial advertising are now being applied to websites. Some sites visually resemble older media and their advertising techniques are obvious. In contrast, other sites are incorporating new types of programming and animation tricks to grab attention and manipulate how people browse the Web. On many sites, you have to click through pages of advertising to find any information. In the worst cases, advertising pops up in a window that covers the page. You have to close this window before you can access information on the site.

Good web design takes you to relevant information within three mouse clicks; in contrast, manipulative designs trap you in the site. In web marketing, *client pull* is the technique of taking over a viewer's browser to take him or her to a website the designer wants the viewer to see. For example, when designers use the HTML programming code called META, the code tells the browser to go to the next page in the site, or to go back and forth among the pages within that site. This simple programming trick can trap you in a website, dragging you deeper and deeper into the site with no apparent escape.

A number of websites are **portal sites,** which are designed to attract mass audiences. These sites include the search engine Yahoo! The home page of a portal site is designed to get people deeper and deeper into the site. Instead of browsing the many different sites on the Internet, these sites want people to stay or "stick" with their site. Therefore, they are designed to keep you locked in the site and they discourage you from leaving. For example, when using Yahoo! as a search engine, you may have to click several times through different screens before you reach a list of links to other sites. While you are clicking, the advertising banner at the top of the page changes to an advertisement that relates to the topic you are searching. Although Yahoo! is a popular search engine, it is also a commercial site that is carefully designed to make you notice its advertising so it can continue to attract sponsors. Understanding how web images and icons are used to manipulate and persuade will make you a more effective web researcher and less likely to be distracted by pushy ploys.

Have you ever missed class because a couple of minutes of web surfing turned into a couple of hours? When doing web research, don't get side-tracked by pushy advertisements and manipulative graphics.

INFORMATION NAVIGATION

A central characteristic of the Web is **hypertext,** which links together information and pages. **Internal links** connect pages within a website. **External links** connect pages from different websites. Links are indicated by text and graphics, including underlined words, phrases, visual icons, and audioclips. As you navigate the Web, the arrow icon changes to a pointing finger when it passes over a link. Selecting different links to navigate information space is a key method for accessing web information.

Navigation and Nontext Features

Graphical browsers add many nontext features to help students navigate the Internet. These include icons, logos, maps, photographs, sounds, and video files. Arrows, buttons, and scrolling bars are visual features used by web designers. These icons enable users to navigate a website and access information.

Navigational aids help students find information on the Web. For instance, an arrow pointing to the right moves one page forward; an arrow pointing to the left moves one page backward (see Figure 4.4). Other navigation features include the title tag, links, navigation icons, and a site map. Every web page has a short and descriptive name. Depending on the browser, this title either appears in the title bar of the window or on the top of the screen. In addition to describing the page, the title is used in indexes and bookmarks. Search engines pick up the title of the site as its default description.

FIGURE 4.4   The Netscape navigation bar helps users navigate hypertextual documents. For example, the forward and backward arrows allow users to move back and forth between web pages and websites.

Netscape Communicator browser window. © 1999 Netscape Communications Corporation. Used with permission. Netscape Communications has not authorized, sponsored, endorsed, or approved this publication and is not responsible for its content.

As previously discussed, hypertext links are underlined text, iconic buttons, or link **anchors** that connect related pieces of information. For instance, links often connect to information that defines a term or provides more information about a particular topic. Similarly, anchors also are used for text navigation because they take readers to sections of a text located on the web page. Links can connect to information located within a single site or they can connect a site to other web pages located anywhere on the global network.

Site maps and indexes can also help users navigate web information. Site maps present a visual representation of the location of information on the site. These maps are often linked to the sections of the site that are represented on the map. An index is an alphabetical listing of the major components of a website. An index or site map provides a quick overview of the site and enables students to locate information more easily.

Evaluation of Content and Navigation Design

Websites should be designed for easy access to relevant information. Sites designed with the intention of making information easily accessible make the amount of content located on the site clearly known. Additionally, the type of information available should be organized into logical units or document groups to help you find the materials that are located on the site. Moreover, the purpose and goals of the site should be clearly articulated. The following are critical content questions to ask when evaluating a site:

1. Is the volume of information contained on the site clearly indicated?
2. Is information on the site grouped into logical units?
3. Does the site have an obvious visual hierarchy? What is the relationship between elements?
4. Does the site indicate which reference materials are located on the site and which ones are on other sites?
5. Are goals articulated for the various areas of the site?
6. Are full texts or only abstracts available?
7. Does the site contain large graphics or visual elements that take time to download?
8. Is the site a digital library collection or a commercial information site?

Many web designers consider oversized graphics the number one sign of poor web design. Graphics should be kept small in size to accommodate a variety of different modem speeds. But there are some exceptions to this rule. Libraries and art collections are now making their collections available online, and large-image collections can take time to download. Digital library collections include the Vatican Library (lcweb.loc.gov/exhibits/vatican/toc.html), the IBM/Andrew Wyeth Project (www.almaden.ibm.com/u/gladney/antiquit.htm), the rare book site at Yale University Beinecke (www.library.yale.edu/beinecke), and the Library of Congress website (www.loc.gov). To protect the copyright of these images, digital library collections frequently place a watermark or embossed logo on the image. Watermarked images indicate that the material on the site is owned by the sponsoring organization. The images are available for viewing, but they cannot be downloaded or printed. Watermarks tend to indicate that the site is presenting original images with a high level of authenticity.

Interactive Functionality Evaluation

The ability to find information easily with several mouse clicks is an indication that a site is designed for interactive functionality. Moreover, well-designed sites have escape links to take you back to the home page of the site. When doing a search, you can end up in the middle of a site. Look for a visual or verbal link to the site's home page to find out more information about who is sponsoring the site and why. If you can't find a link or more information, the information should be checked against another source. The following are critical questions based on design functionality:

1. Does the site follow web conventions? For example, is the text black with blue links?
2. Can you find information quickly with three mouse clicks?
3. Does the site provide its own internal search engine to help you locate information?
4. Can you navigate the site easily?
5. Do the visual images help you better navigate the site?
6. Does the site provide an index or site map?
7. Does every page have a link back to the home page of the site? Can you exit the site?
8. Does each page have an identifying name (or logo), date, and contact email address?

Creating a website that balances interactive functionality and visual design can be difficult. For example, librarians who create sites often have to choose between overloading a page with information or organizing it into units that require additional mouse clicks to access relevant information. Consequently, some highly legitimate sites that contain valuable information are not visually appealing. For example, the Librarian's Index to the Internet (www.lii.org) and the Refdesk (www.refdesk.com) are crowded and unattractive, but the links are carefully chosen and of high quality (see Figure 4.5). On the surface some valuable sites may not attract your attention. You have to read the text carefully or scroll down the screen to use the site functionally.

SUMMARY

In this chapter you read about

- Some basic tips for visual presentation, including
    How color captures attention and conveys meaning
    Using grid formats as a design framework
    The importance of balance in layout

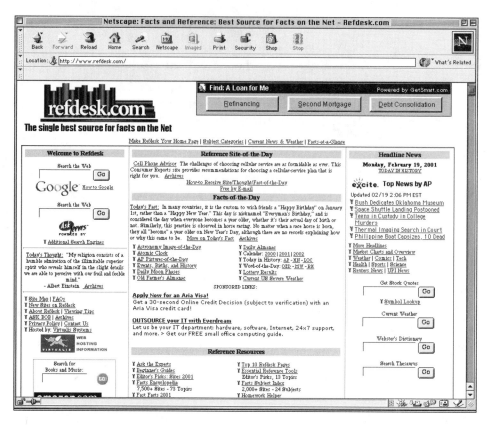

FIGURE 4.5   This site uses one graphic of a bookshelf to orient the user visually to the idea that the site is a good reference source; otherwise the site is filled with text. Text-dominated sites are some of the best reference sites on the Internet.

Reprinted with permission from Bob Drudge, Refdesk.com.

- Points for developing visual savvy, including

  Becoming visually alert

  Identifying a site's visual hierarchy to note emphasis

  Becoming aware of the use of color, animation, and graphics to grab attention

  Becoming aware of manipulation strategies, such as trapping users in a website, that commercial sites use to promote a product or service

- Tips for evaluating information design, including

  Nonverbal navigation elements

  Ascertaining whether the content design of a site is fluff or substantive

  Determining whether the interactive functionality of a site makes it easy to navigate or to find what you are looking for

WEB DESIGN SITES

General

The Virtual Library of WWW Development
WWW.Stars.com/Vlib

Web Page Design for Designers
www.wpdfd.com/wpdhome.htm

Style Guide for Online Hypertext
www.w3.org/Provider/Style/Overview.html

12 Web Page Design Decisions for Business and Organizations
www.wilsonweb.com/articles/12design.htm

What Makes a Good Home Page
www.werbach.com/web/page_design.html

Current Issues in Web Usability (advanced design issues)
www.useit.com/alertbox

Universal Design (Handicap Issues)

Trace: Designing a More Usable Word for All
trace.wisc.edu/world

Examples of Bad Web Design and Design Mistakes

Top 10 Mistakes in Web Design
www.useit.com/alertbox/9605.html

Links to Learning HTML

Teresa's Guide to Learning HTML
www.stanford.edu/~ttorres/Internet/toc.html

Bare Bones Guide to HTML
www.webrach.com/barebones

A Beginner's Guide to HTML
www.ncsa.uiuc.edu//General/Internet/WWW/HTMLPrimerPrintable.html

BIBLIOGRAPHY FOR FURTHER READING

Alexander, Janet E., & Tate, Marsha Ann. (1999). *Web wisdom: How to evaluate and create information quality on the Web.* Mahwah, NJ: Lawrence Erlbaum.

Barry, Ann Marie Seward. (1997). *Visual intelligence: Perception, image, and manipulation in visual communication.* Albany: State University of New York Press.

Berger, Arthur Asa. (1998). *Seeing is believing.* (2nd ed.). Mountain View, CA: Mayfield Press.

Dondis, Donis A. (1973). *A primer for visual literacy.* Cambridge: The MIT Press.

Fox, E. A., & Marchionini, G. (Eds.). (2001, May). Digital libraries. *Association for Computing Machinery, 44*(5), 30–33.

Harrison, T. M., & Stephen, T. (1996). *Computer networking and scholarly communication in the twenty-first-century university.* Albany: State University of New York Press.

McKinley, T. (1997). *From paper to web: How to make information instantly accessible.* San Jose, CA: Adobe Press.

Meggs, Philip B. (1989). *Type and image: The language of graphic design.* New York: Van Nostrand Reinhold.

Peek, R. P., & Newby, G. B. (1996). *Scholarly publishing: The electronic frontier.* Cambridge: The MIT Press.

Waters, C. (1996). *Web concept and design: A comprehensive guide for creating effective web sites.* Indianapolis, IN: New Riders Publishing.

Weinman, L. (1996). *Designing web graphics. 2: How to prepare images and media for the web.* Indianapolis, IN: New Riders Publishing.

White, Jan V. (1990). *Color for the electronic age.* New York: Watson-Guptill Publishers.

CHAPTER 5

Copyright Issues
and the Web

Suppose you worked really hard on a creative project, perhaps wrote a song, made a music video, wrote a short story, or devised a great new computer game. Then, suppose someone came along and took your story, song, video, or game and made it available to anyone and everyone in the world, free of charge, with *no* credit or profit for you. This scenario, of course, would be a good example of what is commonly known as being ripped off! Well, this is what is happening anytime someone downloads or copies information from the Web without giving the author proper credit or citing their source.

"Did you know that according to Billboard, Metallica was the first recording act to sue Napster (for $10 million) for copyright infringement and racketeering? Cliff Burnstein, Metallica's manager said that more than 100 of the band's tracks were made available on Napster." (Billboard, 22 April, 2000)

In the United States, people have the right to be compensated for their creative work. As a result, **copyright** laws have been established to protect every author's intellectual property, including written work, photographs, illustrations, music, and videos. Copyright owners have the exclusive right to copy, distribute, display, and transmit their intellectual property. Permission can be granted to others to use the work, and, in some cases, works are "licensed." Licensing gives others the right to copy and distribute the work within stipulated guidelines. The highly publicized lawsuit against Napster, the popular music-swapping website, argues that the site has been distributing copyrighted material without permission from the copyright owners. As a result, a number of copyright owners have sued Napster. The moral of the story is, if you want to use the creative work of other people, you need to get their permission first. However, the rules of "fair use" constitute an exception to the copyright law.

STAY OUT OF TROUBLE
WITH FAIR-USE GUIDELINES

A fair-use exemption creates a limited set of conditions that allow people to use a copyrighted work without first obtaining permission from the copyright owner. Think about the previous scenario, in which someone took your creative work and distributed it without your permission and without compensation. Wouldn't you be happy to have your work distributed as long as you said it was okay? And, even better, wouldn't it be great to get paid every time someone else used or copied your work? Well, central to the idea of fair use is the notion that your particular use of the work does not divert income from the creator nor influence their potential future income.

Although creative work can be copyright protected, ideas cannot. Therefore, you can write about something someone has already discussed or published. However, using direct quotes or portions of a published work requires giving the author credit. Exemptions under the fair-use interpretation of copyright law are allowed when

- Only a small amount of the copyrighted work is being used

- The small amount used is only an unimportant portion of the entire work and does not define its essence

- The copyright work is being used for educational purposes

- The use of the copyrighted work does not affect the copyright holder's ability to receive income from the work

As you can see, the interpretation of fair use could be tricky. What constitutes educational purposes, for example? How can you tell whether the part of the work you are using is not its essence? Copyright laws are often misunderstood. Many copyright violations take place by those who mistakenly (and often with good intentions) believe that they have the right to make copies.

For example, you paid for an expensive word processing program and installed it on your computer. Your girlfriend or boyfriend asks you to install the program on her/his computer too, *for educational purposes* (i.e., to do homework assignments). Do you think this is a violation of copyright? You might rationalize installing it in this way: "I paid for the program. I want to be able to use it at my significant other's room or apartment. Why shouldn't I install it there, too?" However, you would be in violation of copyright because your installation of that program results in a lack of sale of that program to your main squeeze and a loss of income to the author/ software producer.

Many battles, over many years, fought in U.S. courts, have resulted in some clarification of the gray areas in copyright laws (see the U.S. Copyright Office website at lcweb.loc.gov/copyright/). However, the introduction of digital property, and now the Web, has introduced even grayer areas, and copyright laws have not kept pace with electronic developments. Although most of the information presented through the Web is copyright protected, there is a common belief that messages posted to a public group can be freely copied and distributed. Graphics, sound bites, and text that are copied from websites can be violations of the copyright law. Students creating web pages mistakenly believe that copyright-protected images (such as the Simpsons cartoon characters, or registered company logos) can be cut and pasted into their sites without the creator's permission. These students are wrong!

DON'T ABUSE FAIR USE

Fair use is for educational contexts. Student home pages do not necessarily fall into this category. Students who do not understand how the copyright law works often violate the law without realizing it. For instance, Dale A. Herbeck and Christopher D. Hunter (1997) examined 400 student-authored web pages and discovered that 43 percent of the images used on student pages belonged to someone else. They identified three different ways in which students tend to infringe on other people's copyright:

1. The blatant use of materials that include a visible mark of protection, such as copyright ©, reserved ®, or trademarked TM seals. Examples of this category include cartoon characters and sports logos.

2. The use of materials that are probably protected but do not use a copyright mark. Examples include sports photographs, album and compact disk covers, television characters, and company logos.

3. The use of school or university photographs, seals, logos, shields, and mascots. Although some universities may encourage students to use these

images, they do belong to the university, and students should use these materials with caution.

Several steps can be taken to make sure you are using images properly. The best way to protect oneself is to ask for permission to use the material. Requests can be snail mailed or emailed to the copyright owners. The following sample is a letter of request:

Date

Address [If mailed]

Dear _____:

May I have permission to include your [photograph, illustration, article] in my [project, book, website]. Use of your materials will in no way restrict republication of your material in any other form by you or others authorized by you. A release form is provided below.

I (we) grant the permission requested. The undersigned has the right to grant the permission requested herein and the material does not infringe upon the copyright of other rights of third parties. The undersigned is the owner/author of such materials.

Credit Line to be given: _____

_____

_____

Name _____   Date _____

GUIDELINES FOR OBTAINING PERMISSION

In general, if you want to use someone else's work, you need to get their permission. You should ask for permission in the following cases:

- When using more than 500 words from any single printed source, including all quotations
- When quoting more than 8 percent of a work
- When using any recent artwork or photograph from another source, unless it is a copyright-free image (discussed next)
- When quoting lines from a song or poem

However, some people want their work on the Internet to be shared, and they include permission statements at the end of their work. An example follows:

© 2000, Pat Doe. Permission is granted to freely copy and distribute in electronic or printed form for nonprofit and educational purposes only. The author retains all other rights. If you have any questions, please contact the creator, at patdoe@coldmail.com.

When you see this statement, the materials can be copied and distributed for educational use without directly contacting the owner of the copyright.

COPYRIGHT FOR THE WEB
AND A DIGITAL MILLENNIUM

The Web is a global medium. Different countries have different copyright laws. The Digital Millennium Copyright Act of 1998 makes the Unites States copyright laws conform to two treaties adopted by the World Intellectual Property Organization (WIPO). Basically, all countries have to offer copyright protection to foreign works of **intellectual property** and the protection must be at least as strong as the protection for works in the native country. Moreover, all countries must attempt to prevent using technology to circumvent copyright laws.

What does this mean to you? Information service providers, such as America Online (AOL) and the Microsoft Network, must reject customers that they know engage in copyright infringement. As soon as an Internet service provider receives a complaint of infringement, it must take steps to remove the material from the online service. Under this law, copyright owners also have the right to demand information about the individual who violated copyright.

Copyright Exceptions!

Exceptions to copyright law include works in the public domain and copyright-free clip art. Copyright does not last forever; all works eventually return to the public domain. This means that the images are free for anyone to use. For example, the image of the Mona Lisa falls into this category, and people have used her image in a variety of ways, including adding a mustache! All this is perfectly legal because Mona's image is in the public domain. Works copyrighted before 1978 entered the public domain 75 years after their publication. Between 1978 and 1998, copyright was the life of the author plus 50 years. In 1998, the Sonny Bono Copyright Term Extension Act extended earlier copyright terms by 20 years. As a result of this Act, a large quantity of Disney material that would have gone into the public domain now still belongs to the Disney Company.

Materials for which copyright has expired are considered public domain. Caution! These materials are not current editions, but from much older editions. Examples of public domain materials can be found on the Web:

- *Bartlett's Familiar Quotations* (9th edition) at the Bartleby site, which features public domain works (www.bartleby.com/99/)
- *Roget's Thesaurus* (www.thesaurus.com)

Copyright-free clip art and graphics also constitute exceptions to copyright law because the creators of the work intend for it to be shared. A number of free clip-art services are available on the Web. The good news is that these sites have been linked together into a graphics **web ring** to enable you to click back and forth easily between sites. The bad news is that these sites are filled with annoying advertising banners, windows, and graphics. But after breaking through the clutter, you can find images that do not violate anyone's copyright. Copyright-free art sites include

www.barrysclipart.com/

www.free-clip-art.net

www.clipart.com

www.clipart-graphics.net

www.allclipartsite.com

www.animationcity.net

Materials that were never copyrighted constitute yet another exception to copyright law. These materials include all publications of the U.S. Government Printing Office, which cannot by law be copyrighted. This explains the many versions in print of the Starr Report on former President Clinton and the various versions of the U.S. census.

Web Cheating

Every college and university has rules against plagiarism. **Plagiarism** is using someone else's ideas and words without providing the proper citations or references. When students are caught cheating, consequences may include failing the assignment, failing the course, suspension, and sometimes expulsion. Examples of plagiarism follow:

- Recycling the papers of other students
- Purchasing a paper from a ghost writer
- Copying materials word for word from a book or journal article without citing the source
- Using ideas and passages of texts without acknowledging the author, without using quotation marks, or without including references

Re-mixing or sampling may work in music, but it doesn't apply to writing. Forgetting to place quotation marks and proper citations in your paper is technically a form of plagiarism. For instance, you can't legally just copy and paste sentences from different electronic sources to create a paper of your own.

Computer technology makes it easy to copy information and paste it into another document. It is an easy way for cheaters to plagiarize. However, sometimes even the most honest students working against a deadline can be careless about marking text after a cut and paste. Then they can lose track of where the quotation began and ended. Following are some tips to help you understand when you can and cannot use material copied from the Web for class projects.

DON'TS

- Don't buy papers from an online term-paper mill.
- Don't use a paper from a free term-paper site, such as School Sucks, Other People's Papers, or Evil House of Cheat (see the Tip on page 78).
- Don't cut and paste without marking the text (use **bold** or *italics* to help keep track, or make a print-out of the web page for future reference).

DO'S

- Supply the proper citations and acknowledgments for web sources (see Chapter 6).
- Make sure quotation marks are placed around copied materials.
- Always make note of the web URL for your reference list and in case you need to return to verify material on the original web page.
- Make sure paraphrased materials also are properly acknowledged.

As easy as it is for students to copy papers off the Web, it is easier for professors to find them. In the past, detecting plagiarism required ingenuity, skill, and an amazing memory for text. Today, simply placing a few phrases in a good search engine can identify web cheating.

Let the cheater BEWARE!

Term-paper websites promise to lighten your course load, and some even guarantee that they cannot be detected, all for a mere $7.95 per page. But is it really worth the price? Actually, this is false advertising. New software programs enable professors to catch cheaters, and those choosing to buy online papers may find themselves in deep trouble. For example, Glatt Plagiarism Services (www.plagiarism.com) is a program designed to spot recycled text.

SUMMARY

In this chapter you read about

- Copyright issues and the Web
- Fair-use guidelines and exemptions to copyright, including
    Using a small amount of the copyrighted work
    Using a nonessential portion of the copyrighted work
    Using copyrighted work for educational purposes
    Not affecting the copyright holder's potential income when using the copyrighted material
- Abuses of fair use, including
    Blatantly using materials (such as cartoons) that display a visible copyright or trademark seal
    Using materials that are probably protected (like logos) but do not have a copyright mark
    Using university or college seals or logos without checking to make sure it is permitted
- Guidelines for obtaining permission
    Using more than 500 words from a single source
    Quoting more than 8 percent of a work
    Using artwork or photographs that are not copyright-free clip art
    Quoting lines from a song or poem
- Copyright exceptions for works in the public domain and copyright-free clip art
- Do's and don'ts to avoid web cheating

COPYRIGHT WEBSITES

Copyright Clearance Center
www.copyright.com

Copyright Definitions
www.uflib.ufl.edu/admin/copyright/
  copyright~definitions.htm

Copyright Overview
www.law.cornell.edu/topics/copyright.html

Copyright Legislation
lcweb.loc.gov/copyright/penleg.html

Copyright Resources on the Internet
groton.k12.ct.us/mts/pt2a.htm

Copyright Management Center
www.lupui.edu/~copyinto

Copyright U.S. Code 17
www.law.cornell.edu/uscode/17

U.S. Copyright Office
lcweb.loc.gov/copyright

U.S. Patents and Trademarks Office
www.uspto.gov

World Intellectual Property Organization Treaties
www.wipo.unt

Regents Guide to Understanding Copyright and Educational Fair Use
www.usg.edu/admin/legal/copyright/
  copy.html

Scholarly Electronic Publishing Bibliography
info.lib.uh.edu/sepb/sepb.html

BIBLIOGRAPHY FOR FURTHER READING

Carlson, Scott. (2000). Get ready for an encore of the Napster controversy. *The Chronicle of Higher Education, 47*(2), A51–A54.

Casey, Timothy D. (2000). *ISP liability survival guide: Strategies for managing copyright, SPAM, cache and privacy regulations.* New York: John Wiley & Sons.

Davidson, Hall. (1999). The educator's lean and mean no fat guide to fair use. *Technology and Learning, 20*(2), 58–64.

Ferelli, Mark. (2000). Copyright in cyberspace: Unshaken but not unchanged. *Computer Technology Review, 20*(7), 6.

Fishman, D. (1999). Copyright in a digital world: Intellectual property rights in cyberspace. In S. J. Drucker & G. Gumpert (Eds.), *Real law@virtual space* (pp. 205–226). Cresskill, NJ: Hampton Press.

Fitzpatrick, Eileen. (2000, April 22). Metallica sues Napster & 3 universities. *Billboard, 112* (17), 3.

Fitzpatrick, Eileen. (2000, May 20). RIAA, Metallica wins Napster round, *Billboard, 112*(21), 8–9.

Halbert, Debora J. (1999). *Intellectual property in the information age: The politics of expanding ownership rights.* Westport, CN: Quorum.

Hunter, Christopher D. (1997). Intellectual property and the undergraduate: An analysis of copyright infringement on student web pages. Paper presented at the National Communication Association Convention, Chicago, November 20.

Kleinman, N. (1996). Don't fence me in: Copyright, property, and technology. In L. Strate, R. Jacobson, & S. Gibson (Eds.), *Communication and Cyberspace* (pp. 59–82). Cresskill, NJ: Hampton Press.

Koepsell, David R. (2000). The ontology of cyberspace: Philosophy, law and the future of intellectual property. Chicago: Open Court Publishing.

Moscou, Jim. (1999). Copyright in the digital age. *Editor and Publisher, 132*(50), 32, 34.

Pedzich, Joan. (2001, May 15). Protecting your company's intellectual property: A practical guide to trademarks, copyrights, patents and trade secrets. *Library Journal, 126*(9), 144.

Poynder, Richard. (1999). What price copyright? *Information Today, 16*(11), 14–17.

Winston, Paul D. (2000). Copying this article is strictly prohibited. *Business Insurance, 34*(36), 21.

CHAPTER 6

When and How to Cite Web Sources

Why is it so important to cite your resources properly? Well, one reason is practicality: avoiding copyright infringement (discussed in Chapter 5). A second reason is academics: providing enough information so that interested readers can locate and read an author's original work. Therefore, the purposes of correct **citations** are both to give credit for the origin of ideas or information and to allow readers to find original sources.

After you have gathered your sources, both paper and online, you are all set to write your paper. Part of your paper is the **bibliography** and/or footnotes citing your sources. If you found information on a website, you may be at a loss as to how to cite it. Your professor will most likely require you to use a standard **citation style** such as the Modern Language Association (MLA), Chicago, or American Psychological Association (APA). Manuals describing each of these styles and displaying examples are published. Electronic media, including the Web, email, and Usenet groups, are new enough that only the most recent editions of these style guides (in book form and online) demonstrate how to cite the many different types of electronic resources. This chapter describes some of these and provides examples of the accepted citation styles for citing web resources.

It has been assumed that you understand the basics, or standard conventions, for creating a citation for a bibliography or footnotes. In the Bibliography for Further Reading section at the end of this chapter, the standard style manuals are listed if you need further general assistance with citations. Throughout this chapter, *italics* are used for titles within citations; however, underlining can be used instead if you prefer.

CONSTRUCTING A CITATION

Citations should contain enough specific information about a publication so that someone else can retrieve it. One of the most important things to remember about citing information is that the basic bibliographic elements (e.g., title, author, place of publication, publication date, and location or page numbers) of the citation are the same regardless of the format. However, the order of these elements differs from one format to the next, and electronic sources contain additional elements (for example, URLs and type of medium). In some cases, a citation may not contain every possible element.

To construct a citation, begin by doing the following tasks:

- Locate the web pages or electronic resources you want to refer to in your paper/assignment.
- Find out from your professor what citation style he or she requires. Check your syllabus or course web page to see whether the required style is provided.
- Review this chapter for the style you need and the citation type you are citing.

CITATION STYLES

Citation styles generally fall into two categories: *humanities* (MLA or Chicago) or *scientific* (APA or CBE). Bibliographic listings of electronic sources follow the format for whatever style you are using for print sources.

Scientific Style

Elements for citations in the scientific style are formatted and ordered as follows:

> Author's Last Name, Initial(s). (Date of document [if different from date accessed].) Title of document. Title of complete work [if applicable]. Version or file number [if applicable]. (Edition or revision [if applicable].) Protocol and address, access path, or directories (date of access).

APA has new recommendations for citing online resources. These recommendations are *not* listed in the American Psychological Association Publications Manual, 1994 edition. They are listed at www.apa.org/journals/webref.html and reflected in the examples in this chapter.

Humanities Style

Elements for citations in the humanities style are formatted and ordered as follows:

> Author's Last Name, First Name. "Title of Document." Title of Complete Work [if applicable]. Version or file number [if applicable]. Document date or date of last revision [if different from access date]. Protocol and address, access path, or directories (date of access).

MLA recommends the use of angle brackets (< >) around any URL in type. The idea is to avoid confusion about where the URL begins and ends.

CITING ONLINE NEWSPAPER ARTICLES

SCIENTIFIC STYLE

Newspaper articles from a subscription-based database (e.g., Pro-Quest, NewsBank, or Lexis-Nexis) on the Internet

Author. (Year, month day). Title. *Newspaper Title* [Type of medium], (paging or indicator of length). Available: Supplier/Database name (database identifier or number [if available])/Item or accession number (Access date).

Example

Fairbank, K. (2000, October 24). Frisco, Texas-Based Aerospace Firm Closes. *Dallas Morning News, Knight-Ridder/Tribune Business News* [Online], (3 pp.). Available: NewsBank NewsFile Collection/ Record Number: 094270E7DB1602880E1C7 (2000, October 31).

Newspaper articles from a website (e.g., the newspaper's website) on the Internet

Author. (year, month day). Title. *Newspaper Title* [Type of medium], (paging or indicator of length). Available protocol [if applicable]: site/path/file (access date).

Example

Foster, A. (2000, October 31). New Interpretation of Digital-Copyright Provision Disappoints Scholars. *Chronicle of Higher Education* [Online], 2 pp. Available: http://www.chronicle.com/free/2000/10/ 2000103101t.htm. (2000, October 31).

HUMANITIES STYLE

Newspaper articles from a subscription-based database (e.g., Pro-Quest, NewsBank, Lexis-Nexis) on the Internet

Author. "Article Title." *Newspaper Title*. Date, Edition [if given]: paging or indicator or length. Medium. Information supplier. *Database Name*. File identifier or number. Accession number. Access date.

Example

Fairbank, Katie. "Frisco, Texas-Based Aerospace Firm Closes." *Dallas Morning News, Knight-Ridder/Tribune Business News,* 24 Oct. 2000: 3 pp. Online. NewsBank. *NewsFile Collection.* Record Number: 094270E7DB1602880E1C7. 31 Oct. 2000.

Newspaper articles from a website (e.g., the newspaper's website) on the Internet

Author. "Article Title." *Newspaper Title.* Date, Edition [if given]: paging or indicator or length. Medium. Available Protocol [if applicable]: site/path/file. access date

Example

Foster, Andrea L. "New Interpretation of Digital-Copyright Provision Disappoints Scholars." *Chronicle of Higher Education.* 31 Oct. 2000: 2 pp. Online. Available: http://www.chronicle.com/free/2000/10/ 2000103101t.htm. 2000 October 31.

CITING ONLINE MAGAZINE ARTICLES

Generally, the terms *magazine* and *journal* are interchangeable. However, when it comes to scholarly writing and citing your sources, there is a difference. Journals are of a scholarly nature. Journal articles are in depth and often reviewed in depth by experts before being accepted for publication by the journal editors. Articles may be peer reviewed or, more rigorously, blind reviewed, a process whereby reviewers do not know who the author is and the author does not know who the reviewers are. Magazines feature articles on more popular topics that go into less depth and are usually written in a lighter style that is easy to read.

SCIENTIFIC STYLE

Magazine articles from a subscription database on the Internet

Author. (Year, month day). Title. *Magazine Title* [Type of medium], *volume*(issue) [if given], paging or indicator of length. Available:

Supplier/Database name (Database identifier or number [if available])/Item or accession number (Access date).

Example

Lobb, W. (1992, August). The players (US Olympic marathoners). *Runner's World* [Online], *27*(8), 70–74. Available: Gale/Infotrac Web Expanded Academic ASAP International Ed./Article A12450529 (2000, Nov. 5).

Magazine articles from a website (e.g., the magazine's website) on the Internet

Author. (Year, month day). Title. *Magazine Title*. [Type of medium], *volume* [if given], paging or indicator of length. Available Protocol [if applicable]: site/path/file (Access date).

Example

Machrone, B. (2000, October 19). TOS your cookies. *PC Magazine*. [Online], 2 pp. Available: http://www.zdnet.com/pcmag/stories/opinions/0,7802,2641793,00.html (2000 Nov 5).

HUMANITIES STYLE

Magazine articles from a subscription database on the Internet

Author. "Article Title." *Magazine Title*. Date: paging or indicator of length. Medium. Information supplier. *Database Name*. File identifier or number. Accession number. Access date.

Example

Lobb, Welles. "The Players (US Olympic Marathoners)." *Runner's World*. August 1992: 70–74. Online. Available: Gale. *Infotrac Web Expanded Academic ASAP International Ed*. Article A12450529. 5 Nov. 2000.

Magazine articles from a website (e.g., the magazine's website) on the Internet

Author. "Article Title." *Magazine Title*. Date: paging or indicator of length. Medium. Available Protocol [if applicable]: site/path/file. Access date.

Example

Machrone, Bill. "TOS Your Cookies." *PC Magazine*. August 1992: 2 pp. Online. Available: http://www.zdnet.com/pcmag/stories/opinions/ 0,7802,2641793,00.html. 5 Nov 2000.

CITING ONLINE JOURNALS

SCIENTIFIC STYLE
Journal articles from a subscription database on the Internet

Author. (Year). Title. *Journal Title* [Type of medium], *volume*(issue), paging or indicator of length. Available: Supplier/Database name (Database identifier or number [if available])/Item or accession number (access date).

Example

Hays, S. M. (1996). Golden nematodes are anything but. *Agricultural Research* [Online], 44(4), 16–17. Available:Gale/Infotrac Web Expanded Academic ASAP International Ed./Article A18347641 (1999, June 5).

Journal articles from a website (e.g., the journal's website) on the Internet

Author. (year). Title. *Journal Title* [Type of medium], *volume*(issue), paging or indicator of length. Available Protocol [if applicable]: site/path/file (access date).

Example

Brewer, J. S. (1999). Short-term effects of fire and competition on growth and plasticity of the yellow pitcher plant, Sarracenia alata (Sarraceniaceae). *American Journal of Botany* [Online], 86, 16 pages. Available: www.amjbot.org/cgi/content/full/86/9/1264 (1999, June 5).

HUMANITIES STYLE

Journal articles from a subscription database on the Internet

Author. "Article Title." *Journal Title.* Volume.Issue(Year): paging or indicator of length. Medium. Information supplier. *Database Name.* File identifier or number. Accession number. Access date.

Example

Hays, Sandy Miller. "Golden Nematodes Are Anything But." *Agricultural Research.* 44.4(1996): 16–17. Online. Available: Gale. *Infotrac Web Expanded Academic ASAP International Ed.* Article A18347641. 1999, June 5.

Journal articles from a website (e.g., the journal's website) on the Internet

Author. "Article Title." *Journal Title.* Volume.Issue (Year): paging or indicator of length. Medium. Available Protocol [if applicable]: site/path/file. Access date.

Example

Brewer, J. Stephen. "Short-Term Effects of Fire and Competition on Growth and Plasticity of the Yellow Pitcher Plant, Sarracenia alata (Sarraceniaceae)." *American Journal of Botany* 86 (1999): 16 pages. Online. Available: http://www.amjbot.org/cgi/content/full/86/9/1264 (1999, June 5).

CITING DISCUSSION LIST ENTRIES
FROM EMAIL AND FROM LIST ARCHIVES

SCIENTIFIC STYLE

• Discussion list entry from an email account

AUTHOR. (Year, Month day). Subject of message. *Discussion List* [Type of medium]. Available Email: DISCUSSION LIST@e-mail address [Access date].

Note: Author's login name, in uppercase, is given as the first element.

Example

LINDA BARR. (2000, August 29). Call number dates for UMI reprinted dissertations. *Autocat* [Online]. Available Email: AUTOCAT@listserv.acsu.buffalo.edu [2000, September 3].

• Discussion list entry from the list archives

Author. (Year, Month day). Subject of message. *Discussion List* [Type of medium]. Available Email: LISTSERV@e-mail address/Get (Access date).

Example

LINDA BARR. (2000, August 29). Call number dates for UMI reprinted dissertations. *Autocat* [Online]. Available Email: AUTOCAT@listserv. acsu.buffalo.edu/Get 072096 (2000, September 3).

HUMANITIES STYLE

• Discussion list entry from an email account

AUTHOR. "Subject of Message." Date. Online posting. Discussion List. Available Email: DISCUSSION LIST@e-mail address. Access date.

Note: Author's login name, in uppercase, is given as the first element.

Example

LINDA BARR. "Call number dates for UMI reprinted dissertations." Aug. 29 2000. Online posting Autocat. Available Email: AUTOCAT@listserv.acsu.buffalo.edu. Sept. 3 2000.

Discussion list entry from the list archives

Author. "Subject of Message." Date. Online posting. Discussion List. Available Email: LISTSERV@e-mail address/Get. Access date.

Note: Author's login name, in uppercase, is given as the first element.

Example

LINDA BARR. "Call number dates for UMI reprinted dissertations." Aug. 29 2000. Online posting Autocat. Available Email: AUTOCAT@listserv.acsu.buffalo.edu/Get autocat 072096. Sept. 3 2000.

CITING EMAIL MESSAGES

SCIENTIFIC STYLE

Sender (Sender's email address). (Year, Month day). Subject of message. Email to recipient (Recipient's email address).

Example

Radford, Marie (mradford@prodigy.net). (2000, July 25). Status of project. Email to Linda Barr (lbarr@uvi.edu).

HUMANITIES STYLE

Sender (Sender's email address). "Subject of Message." Email to recipient (Recipient's email address). Date of message.

Example

Radford, Marie (mradford@prodigy.net). "Status of project." Email to Linda Barr (lbarr@uvi.edu). 25 July 2000.

CITING GOVERNMENT RESOURCES

In the summer of 2000, the U.S. Government Printing Office (GPO) stated that web-only versions of previously printed documents produced by and for government agencies would begin being published. The GPO is rapidly phasing out the costly printing of government documents in favor of delivering them electronically whenever possible. As you might imagine, the U.S. government puts out an incredible amount of information each year. (Think about, for example, the amount of information distributed by the Bureau of the Census, the IRS, the U.S. Congress, and our court systems.) This radical change in the way our government is distributing information makes it important to understand how to cite these electronic documents. What follows are guidelines based on APA style.

Government publications are written by or for federal agencies and printed, not published, by the GPO. These publications do not follow a standard title page arrangement whether on paper or online. The basic form of a document retrieved via online databases or the Internet should include the author, title and edition, type of medium, date, availability of directories and files as needed. Remember, the purpose of the citation is to allow readers to locate the source. Therefore, the citation should contain enough specific information about the publication to retrieve it. Use minimal punctuation because periods or commas may be mistaken for part of an electronic address. The scientific style (APA) is the main style for government documents.

SCIENTIFIC STYLE

Author. Title (edition), TYPE OF MEDIUM. Date of publication. Supplier. Available: Uniform Resource Locator (Access date).

Example

U.S. Bureau of the Census. HIV/AIDS surveillance data base. ONLINE. 2000. Census Bureau. Available: http://www.census.gov/ipc/www/ hivaidsd.html (5 Nov. 2000).

SUMMARY

In this chapter you read about

- How to cite web resources using citation formats for both humanities and scientific styles
- How to cite online newspaper articles
- How to cite online magazine articles
- How to cite online journal articles
- How to cite discussion list entries from email and from list archives
- How to cite email messages
- How to cite government resources

WEB RESOURCES

American Psychological Association Recommended Electronic Reference Formats
www.apastyle.org/elecref.html

Online Citation Styles Index
www.bedfordstmartins.com/online/citex.html

Columbia Guide to Online Style (CGOS)
www.columbia.edu/cu/cup/cgos/idx_basic.html

Internet Public Library, Citing Electronic Resources
www.ipl.org/ref/QUE/FARQ/netciteFARQ.html

APA Citation Style, Long Island University, B. Davis Schwartz Memorial Library
www.liunet.edu/cwis/cwp/library/workshop/citapa.htm

Frequently Asked Questions about MLA Style
www.mla.org/www_mla_org/style/style_main.asp

Style Sheets for Citing Internet and Electronic Resources: Humanities (MLA and Chicago), Scientific (APA and CBE), and History (Turabian)
www.lib.berkeley.edu/TeachingLib/Guides/Internet/Style.html

Uncle Sam—Brief Guide to Citing Government Publications
www.lib.memphis.edu/gpo/citeweb.htm

BIBLIOGRAPHY FOR FURTHER READING

The Bluebook: A uniform system of citation. (16th ed.). (1996). Cambridge: Harvard Law Review Association.

Chicago manual of style. (14th ed.). (1993). Chicago: University of Chicago Press.

Garner, Diane, & Smith, Diane H. (1984). *The complete guide to citing government documents: A manual for writers and librarians.* Bethesda, MD: Congressional Information Service.

Gibaldi, Joseph. (1998). *MLA style manual and guide to scholarly publishing.* (2nd ed.). New York: Modern Language Association of America.

Li, Xia, & Crane, Nancy B. (1996). *Electronic styles: A handbook for citing electronic information.* (2nd ed.). Medford, NJ: Information Today.

Patrias, Karen. (1991). *National library of medicine recommended formats for bibliographic citation.* Bethesda, MD: National Library of Medicine.

Publication manual of the American Psychological Association. (4th ed.). (1994). Washington, DC: American Psychological Association.

Glossary

●●

Anchors. Linked points on the same web page.

AND operator. A Boolean operator used to *narrow* searches. When used in web searches, *AND* requires that both terms be present to be retrieved. For example, *math AND calculus* only returns sites with both terms.

Banner ads. Advertisements placed on web pages that often appear as long horizontal boxes placed at the top of a page.

Bibliography. A list of references and/or additional readings usually located at the end of a research paper.

Boolean operators. The words AND, OR, or NOT (always capitalized) that can be used to construct search strategies. The most common Boolean Operators are AND, OR, and NOT. These connect the terms you are searching and are used to narrow or broaden a search. For example, child AND violence, narrows your search to mean that you are looking for articles or web pages including both terms; child OR children broadens your search to mean that you are looking for articles or web pages including either term; violence NOT television narrows your search to mean that you want to exclude articles or web pages containing the second term.

Browsers. Programs that interpret and display documents formatted in the hypertext markup language (HTML).

Citation. Bibliographic information about a particular document. Generally citations include the author, title, publisher, place of publication, and date. Citations for web resources also include additional elements, such as the URL and date accessed.

Citation style. A proscribed method of ordering the elements of a citation. Common citation styles include MLA (Modern Language Association), APA (American Psychological Association), and Chicago styles.

Copyright. The exclusive right to sell, publish, or distribute a creative work or intellectual property.

Domain names. Names that identify the type of organization operating the Internet server. The five generic domains are gov, edu, com, net, and org. Additionally, domain names can include country codes, for example *ca* for Canada and *us* for United States.

Extensions.   The three letters added to a file name to indicate the type of file. At the end of Internet URL addresses extensions refer to the Internet domain name, for example, .com = commercial, .net = host or gateway, .edu = educational organization, .gov = governmental, .org = nonprofit organization.

External links.   Internet links that connect pages from different websites.

False hit (also, false drop).   A site returned by a search engine that is not relevant to your search topic. This situation is common with keyword searches, especially when the keyword has more than one meaning. For example, you may be looking for information about JAVA, the programming language. You type in the term *JAVA*. The search engine returns a list of sites, including those about the programming language JAVA (*hits*), but also those about the Indonesian country (*false hits*) and even sites that have the term JAVA used as a slang term for coffee (*false hits*).

Graphical user interfaces (GUIs).   The use of icons instead of typed commands to execute computer instructions. This type of interface design uses windows, pull-down menus, visual metaphors (such as the desktop), and a mouse. The two major GUIs are Windows and Macintosh.

Hyperlink.   Usually called links, these are areas of the web page that are linked or connected to a different page or part of the same page. Selecting a link will take you to a different piece of information. Links can be images, words, pictures, or phrases.

Hypertext.   Nonsequential reading and writing. Information is connected or linked together and viewed in an associative way instead of as a linear sequence.

Hypertext markup language (HTML).   Codes used to format World Wide Web documents. Individual codes define the hierarchy and nature of the various components of the document, and specify hypertext links. For example, <title>Title</title> would show the title of a Web document or page.

Hypertext transport protocol (HTTP).   A communication protocol designed for web browsers that allows users to move from web page to web page around the World Wide Web.

Integrated search engines. Search engines that run searches on multiple search engines and return an integrated list of sites displayed in a single list with duplicates removed.

Intellectual property. The creative work of an individual or groups of individuals, including the creation of written work, artwork, and software programs.

Internal links. Internet links that connect pages within a website.

Meta–search engines. Search engines that run searches on other search engines and directories. Can return results that are integrated (sites displayed in a single list with duplicate sites removed) or nonintegrated (sites displayed in separate lists with duplicate sites remaining).

Metasites (also, subject directories). Collections of high-quality web pages organized into subject categories, usually by human indexers who are librarians or subject specialists.

Nonintegrated search engines. Search engines that run searches on multiple search engines and return a list of sites displayed in separate lists with duplicate sites remaining.

NOT operator. A Boolean operator used for *exclusion*. When used in web searches, *NOT* requires that one term not be present. For example, *math* **NOT** *calculus* returns sites with the term *math*, but not the term *calculus*.

OR operator. A Boolean operator used to *broaden* searches. When used in web searches, *OR* requires that either term be present to be retrieved. For example, *math* **OR** *mathematics* returns sites with either term or both terms.

Plagiarism. Using someone else's ideas and words without providing the proper citations or references.

Portal sites. Web traffic control sites that are designed to attract users before they visit other sites on the Internet. They provide gateways to accessing Internet information.

Precision. A measure of the effectiveness of your search. How many on-target/on-topic sites did the search engine find in relation to the total number of sites found?

Push technology. Technology that enables advertising messages to be pushed onto web users. This is often done through pop-up windows and animated banner advertisements.

Relevance.   The degree to which the sites you found are judged by you to be on target, that is, actually about your topic.

Search engines.   Software tools that allow web users to find information on the network. Presently, search engines are text based, and information is located through key word searches.

Subject directory.   See *metasite.*

Uniform Resource Locator (URL).   The address that defines the route to a file on the Web or any other Internet facility. URLs are typed into the browser to access web pages, and URLs are embedded within the pages themselves to provide the hypertext links to other pages. For example, www.ablongman.com is a URL.

Visual hierarchy.   A group of visual (and verbal) elements arranged according to emphasis. Emphasis is achieved with contrast, stressing the relative importance, separation, or connection of graphic elements.

Web rings.   Sites with a common interest that band together into linked circles to enable people to find them more quickly and easily.

INDEX